MUTINY AT THE CURRAGH

L.E.A.

SIR EDWARD CARSON

MUTINY AT THE CURRAGH

BY

A. P. RYAN

I enter upon a time rich in catastrophes, full of
civic strife, a time when even peace had horrors
of its own.'—TACITUS, *Histories*

'Boys, oh boys, 'tis then there was ructions.'
Ballad of Lanigan's Ball

LONDON
MACMILLAN & CO LTD
NEW YORK · ST MARTIN'S PRESS
1956

PREFACE

THE events described in these pages belong to a transitional period of history. They move in that tricky twilight of the comparatively recent past which is beyond the active memory of most people but still vividly recalled by a few. This gives a chronicler special advantages and some handicaps. He is able to hear from the lips of some of those engaged, in major or minor capacities, in helping to shape events why they acted as they did. He has available much unpublished written evidence. On the other hand, a good deal of the published material, coming as it does from partisans, is controversial. What happened at the Curragh in the spring of 1914 — and how it had been led up to in the years immediately preceding — has not yet wholly faded into the calmer perspectives of history. Talking to many people, military and civilian, who have not forgotten how fiercely they took sides, is to be impressed by the explosive qualities of this theme.

I have used, in tackling it, the three kinds of evidence — verbal testimony, unpublished documents and newspapers, periodicals and books. A Bibliography of Published Sources is given on p. 213 at the end of this book.

Wherever possible I have allowed those who took leading parts in these events to speak for themselves. General Sir Hubert Gough, who commanded the Cavalry Brigade which was the centre of this affair, has given me invaluable help. His memory is keen, his judgment decisive and bluntly emphatic, and his private papers, including much written in the heat of the fray, are voluminous. I am most grateful to him for having placed all these at my disposal.

v

Sir James Fergusson of Kilkerran has been no less kind in permitting me to use the very full unpublished records kept by his father, the late General Sir Charles Fergusson, who commanded the 5th Division in Ireland, and whose coolly effective handling of an ugly situation has earned him far less credit than he deserved. Mrs. Crawford, the widow of Colonel F. H. Crawford, C.B.E., who organized and executed the gun-running into Ulster, has been good enough to permit me freely to use her husband's graphic, privately printed account of his exploits.

Sir Maurice and Lady Violet Bonham Carter gave me access to the Asquith papers, which are being kept, on behalf of Balliol College, in the Bodleian Library. Sir Harold Nicolson, with his usual generosity, saved me from research that I would otherwise have made into the part played by George V.

Mr. Amery who, as a young M.P. with close military associations, was in the thick of the battle, told me what he recalled and allowed me to consult his many relevant files of memoranda and letters.

Professor Denis Gwynn, the biographer of Redmond, gave me the benefit of his intimate familiarity with Irish history and put me in touch with other Irishmen who were 'in the picture'.

Lord Beaverbrook, as Mr. Max Aitken, was host to the Prime Minister, Mr. Asquith, and to the Leader of the Opposition, Mr. Bonar Law, when they had reason to meet informally and without publicity. He was good enough to stir his vivid recollections for me.

Lord Mottistone searched the papers of his father who, as Sir John Seely, was Secretary of State for War in 1914, and allowed me to see them. Sir Herbert Creedy, in 1914 and for so many years afterwards in the centre of things at the War Office, gave me his shrewd, dispassionate impressions of Whitehall before, during and after the Curragh.

Brigadier-General Sir Harvey Kersley, who was Sir Hubert Gough's Brigade Major, and Mr. Kenneth Lyon, who was Private Secretary to the Adjutant-General, Sir John Ewart, and Brigadier Lord Malise Graham, A.D.C. to General Sir Charles Fergusson, have kindly helped me. Mrs. Howell, whose memoir of her husband, Brigadier-General Philip Howell, convincingly gives the atmosphere of the Curragh scene in which she shared, has thrown some interesting conversational sidelights on it.

My thanks are also due to Mr. D. W. King of the War Office Library, Commander Kemp, R.N. (retd.), of the Admiralty Library, and Wing Commander E. Bentley Beauman of the Royal United Service Institution Library, and to the Librarians of *The Times*, of the *Daily Telegraph* (including the films of the *Morning Post*), of the *News Chronicle* (including the files of the *Westminster Gazette*) and of Chatham House. The staff of the London Library were, as is their custom, indefatigable in piloting me through the catacombs in which the files of periodicals are stored in St. James's Square.

None of those for whose help and interest I am sincerely grateful is in any way responsible for the assessment given here of this phase of political history.

A. P. RYAN

LONDON, 1956

CONTENTS

ILLUSTRATIONS

SICILIAN WESTMINSTER

IN the middle of January 1912 the British Prime Minister, Asquith, who was spending a well-earned holiday in the Mediterranean, wrote home to his wife, Margot, that the Sicilians were a semi-barbarous race, who lived like the Irish and whose shocking roads had made short work of the Rolls-Royce.

The Irish were very much on Asquith's mind at this moment. The Liberal Government, which he led, had been forced to the conclusion that at long last it must put some measure of Home Rule for Ireland through Parliament. Asquith approached this task confident that it could be done, and without enthusiasm. He knew that the Liberals and the Irish members who supported them were in for some stormy sessions in the House of Commons and for another burst of resentful opposition in the House of Lords. But their lordships had lately been hamstrung and shorn of their constitutional strength; they had lost the right to reject indefinitely a Bill passed by the Lower House. Refreshed by southern sunshine, Asquith expected to begin operations in the spring and to get the Royal Assent for his Home Rule Act before he next went to the country at a general election.

The events of the next two and a half years were to dumbfound him and other political prophets brought up in the Victorian and Edwardian traditions of parliamentary procedure in what they believed to be an orderly, broad-minded democracy. Before these two and a half years were out, the British people were to learn a number of

surprising and unexpected things about their own psychology. They were to see a private army raised to defy the
will of Parliament, drilling openly, effectively armed and
led by the leaders of one of the two great political parties.
The Front Opposition Bench was to glory in its support of
rebellion, and to use language in and out of the House that,
in normal circumstances, would have landed the speakers
in gaol. High dignitaries of the churches were to vie with
the statesmen in blessing well-organized preparations for
using force to defy the constitution.

Fundamental principles on which British public life
is founded were to be called in question. Was there a
limit to the right of a duly elected majority of members to
impose a law on a conscientiously objecting minority?
Were there any circumstances in which such a minority
would be morally justified in taking the law into their own
hands? Both these questions were asked and answered in
the affirmative by men of the most impeccably responsible
political backgrounds. The King, George V — still, in
1912, an underestimated personality — was to be dragged
into the argument. He, too, was to be faced with awkward,
embarrassing and almost unprecedented questions. Was
it not his duty, in certain circumstances, to override his
ministerial advisers and to dissolve Parliament against their
wishes? Again an answer in the affirmative came from
quarters that might have been expected to take a most
conservative view of monarchical responsibility.

As the storm rose and the volunteer citizens were
shaped more and more efficiently into an armed formation,
mass meetings were held to encourage them in England as
well as in Ireland. The technique of whipping up crowd
enthusiasm, with which Hitler made a later generation
familiar, was given a pre-view in a Britain on the eve of
the Kaiser's war. The Government, at first contemptuous
and then alarmed, found itself compelled to consider the
use of the armed forces to maintain the authority of the

lawful civil power. Precedents for turning out the troops were sought and found as recently as the coal strikes in South Wales and as far back in history as the Chartist riots and the disorders at the time of the Reform Bill.

At last, and reluctantly, Asquith's Cabinet nerved itself to move troops, and as soon as it did so it was confronted with what was widely, though inaccurately, described as a mutiny. A classic confusion of orders, the responsibility for which was shared between cabinet ministers and generals, led to the officers of three regiments of cavalry showing their preference for sacrificing their careers rather than marching in step with their civil superiors. A cry of 'the army versus the people' went up, and the cavalry were accused of being arrogant, aristocratic play-boys who behaved like Conservative politicians rather than disciplined holders of the King's Commission. But a large body of opinion in and out of Parliament, and not confined to men and women of strong political convictions, supported them.

The issue was still further complicated by a rival cry that went up that the Government had hatched a wicked plot. The level-headed Asquith was popularly acquitted of being one of the conspirators. He was held to have been duped or, at least, hurried off his feet by his First Lord, Winston Churchill, and his Secretary of State for War, Sir John Seely (later Lord Mottistone). The charge was that, under cover of moving troops for the blameless purpose of preventing ammunition depots being raided by gangsters masquerading as patriots, a section of the Cabinet had deliberately set out to provoke disorder. They were accused of having nefariously planned a combined naval and military operation which would have involved the landing of large bodies of sailors and soldiers in Ireland and, by thus trailing the coat, inciting the private army to action.

Denial, emphatic but less specific and detailed than the

prosecution demanded, was made at the time. The full facts were not established to the satisfaction of the average bewildered citizen, and the 'plot' is believed in to this day by some survivors of the pre-first-world-war parliament.

As these events followed quickly on one another, they were watched with characteristic thoroughness and with no less characteristic misunderstanding of the fundamentals of the British way of life by German diplomats and service chiefs. It has been said that Germany would not have risked her invasion of Belgium had she not been satisfied that Britain had her hands tied by a civil war looming up in Ireland. This is an exaggeration. Germany would have acted as she did even had all been quiet on the Irish front, but the absence of quiet there was certainly agreeable and encouraging to warmongers on the continent.

How Asquith would have got out of his difficulties if war had not descended like a *diabolus ex machina* and swept the petty drama of Ireland off the stage is very far from being clear. Fruitless negotiations to settle the Irish question, centring on Buckingham Palace, were being held when, in Grey's phrase, the lights went out. Through the darkness, and unnoticed by a Britain struggling for survival in the clash for world power, dim figures continued to move restlessly to and fro in Ireland. They were the ultimate heirs and beneficiaries of the extraordinary anarchy of these two and a half years. The British political vendetta of 1912 to 1914 prepared the way for the 1916 Easter Rising and for the setting up of the Irish Republic.

Quite apart from the Irish issue, and in many ways more interesting, is the temporary loss of balance, of the genius for compromise and of the instinctive turning in times of constitutional stress to the safety of moderation that marks this phase of British politics. It almost seems to an observer, reading the language that was used from the Front Benches, on platforms and in the press, that leaders on all sides had grown weary of the long peace. There is more to life, they seemed to be saying, than can be got into a ballot-box. The forty years that have since elapsed have been so loud with ugly echoes of this reaction against Victorian stability that the wild talk and wild acts of 1912 to 1914 sound like the opening chorus to a tragedy. Between the angry, interminable columns of Hansard, there rise to the eyes the lines of a contemporary poet, G. K. Chesterton :

> Likelier across these flats afar,
>   These sulky levels smooth and free,
> The drums shall crash a waltz of war
>   And Death shall dance with Liberty ;
> Likelier the barricades shall blare
>   Slaughter below and smoke above,
> And death and hate and hell declare
>   That men have found a thing to love.

Asquith's most extreme opponents would have been horrified had they been told that what they were saying arose partly from boredom in the depths of their unconscious selves with law, order and the hitherto largely unquestioned processes of democratic procedure.   But their words betray them. Asquith's Sicilian comparison was more far-reaching and relevant than he thought when he wrote to his wife. A Sicilian streak was to be revealed in Westminster as in Ulster ; to trace it from the beginning of 1912 until the outbreak of the 1914 war is the purpose of this book.

B

CHAPTER I

BACKGROUND TO THE VENDETTA

NO parliament has suffered more from an embarrassment of riches in the shape of brilliant men and none has been more bad-tempered than the one opened in state by the King on February 14, 1912. A ministry of all the intellectual and oratorical talents was faced by a glowering opposition well equipped to hold office and starved for it. Much more than party rivalry had, in the past few years, upset the traditional British instinct for basically good-humoured give-and-take. Members on Front and Back Benches and in both Houses were licking their wounds and spoiling for another fight. A social revolution had begun and had stirred the depths of feeling normally left unruffled and unplumbed in Westminster.

Through hot summer nights in 1911 Parliament had sat so angrily that a war to the knife and fork had become a reality in Fifth-Georgian London. Hostesses had to be careful about mixing guests on opposing political sides. And when English men and women allow public differences to strain social relations, it is a sign that nerves are on edge as well as points of view in conflict. Never could a more unfortunate moment have been chosen for dropping yet another match into that political powder magazine, the Irish question.

But Asquith and his colleagues had no choice in the matter. The two electoral battles they had won since their famously sweeping victory of 1906 had inflicted sad casualties on the ranks of radical progress. The Government was now in the position, always irksome to high command, of being unable to carry on a prosperous campaign without the support of allies, and these, as is the way of allies, were demanding their reward for loyalty. Had Redmond and his Irish Nationalist supporters refused to go into the lobbies on the Liberal side, Asquith's ministry would have fallen. It had been made aware of this ugly fact in the course of the bitter struggles over Lloyd George's Budget and the hamstringing of the House of Lords.

The Irish Nationalists felt no particular enthusiasm for the attack on aristocratic landlords and other comfortable citizens which was a key point in Liberal policy. They had voted for it in order to be entitled to claim their price with as little delay as possible. Too long, they felt and, from their angle, with good reason, had they been kept waiting within sight of the land promised a generation earlier by Gladstone. Redmond, writing on the eve of the great battles, now in 1912 recent and vivid history, had made no bones about it. 'Unless an official declaration on the question of Home Rule be made,' he had told John Morley, 'not only will it be impossible for us to support Liberal candidates in England, but we will most unquestionably have to ask our friends to vote against them . . . as you know very well, the opposition of Irish voters in Lancashire, Yorkshire and other places, including Scotland, would most certainly mean the loss of many seats.' Nothing could be plainer than that.

The evil hour for the Liberal Party had been postponed by the strength in which it was returned at the 1906 General Election. Gladstone's dream of 'a party totally independent of the Irish vote' had then come transiently true. But it was too good to last. 'The longer it is before the Irish question interrupts the swing in our direction,' John Morley had reflected, nervously and prophetically, 'the better for all of us.' What had now interrupted the swing was the reduction of the House of Lords to a constitutional cipher. So long as their Lordships could throw out a Home Rule Bill, depriving it of any chance of getting on to the Statute Book, a Liberal Cabinet could plead with the Irish for delay; they could appeal to the dismal precedent of Gladstone's failure over his second Home Rule Bill, which passed the House of Commons and was then rejected by the still entrenched Upper House.

Asquith had, at that time, while he was still a young statesman, coined a phrase to describe the suicidal attempts of his grand old leader to grant Ireland some sort of self-government. It was, he had declared, a barren exercise in 'ploughing the sands'. But, now, Asquith had lived to harrow the Lords, and the sands were fertilized with coronets. Something must be done to satisfy the not inexhaustible patience of Redmond. But what exactly would satisfy him without, in the process, restoring the fortunes of the Conservative party and weakening Liberal unity was far from clear. An attempt had been made, earlier in the life of the Government, to placate the Nationalists with an 'Irish Councils Bill'. But this 'jejune little sop', as Sir Harold Nicolson has called it, was rejected out of hand. A full-scale Home Rule Bill was inevitable. Cabinet ministers disagreed on the particulars of what such a Bill should include and they shared a common lack of enthusiasm for it in any shape. There was no one among them who felt the messianic enthusiasm of Gladstone for Irish affairs. They would, had they dared, have put off facing Parliament on this distasteful issue until the Greek Calends.

It was not even as if Ireland were in the state of discontent and murderous disorder to which earlier generations of British politicians had been accustomed. On the contrary, she was quieter and less distressful than she had been within the memory of living men. For once in a way the Irish had nothing, materially speaking, to grumble about. And, what is no less remarkable, for once in a way they were not grumbling — outside Westminster and, of course, the United States. There, itinerant Irish politicians could still count on Americans of Celtic stock to supply them lavishly with dollars and to cheer them as often as they indulged in the time-honoured game of twisting the British lion's tail. Redmond had assured a receptive audience of Kellys and Murphys in Chicago that 'there is not an Irishman in America today, in whose veins good red blood is flowing, who would not rejoice to hear that a German army was marching in triumph across England from Yarmouth to Milford Haven'.

But Redmond would have been as horrified had such a thing happened as his Chicago hearers would have been baffled had they been asked to say where Yarmouth and Milford Haven lie on the map. He was an Irish gentleman, friendly to Britain and, when war with Germany came, he did his loyal best to bring in all Irishmen of military age on the British side, and he might well have succeeded had not Kitchener prevented him. That he let himself go in this rhetorical style as soon as he crossed the Atlantic is significant. For it is a reminder of how sensitive even the most sober politicians are — and few politicians have been more sober than Redmond was — to atmosphere. The American Irish of that day were still living in the past of Famine and Fenianism; Redmond, instinctively and, perhaps, with tongue in cheek, played up to their mood. It was a mood no longer contemporary in Britain or Ireland on the verge of yet another Home Rule debate. But it was quickly to be revived. The past was to live again in Anglo-Irish politics and British ministers and ex-ministers were soon to express themselves in language which made Mr. Redmond's oratory in Chicago sound common form.

How furiously the battle was about to rage could not be foreseen by anyone at the beginning of 1912. But the Irish question, whenever it arose down the centuries, had always raised more dust than had been expected and the one invariable ending to each attempt to answer it was that the solution was left for the future to find.   Irish patriots blamed British aggression for these recurrent failures, and public opinion in Britain blamed the incorrigibly unreasonable, tread-on-the-tail-of-my-coat Irish temperament. So long as peasants were starving in the bogs, landlords being sniped at from behind stone fences and cattle being maimed, John Bull recognized that it was his duty to do something about it.   But, so far as he could see in 1912, there was nothing urgently practical for him to do.

He had gone far towards settling the land troubles that were at the root of the violent disorders that had persisted until late Victorian days.   Thanks largely to a romantic figure in Balfour's last Conservative Government — George Wyndham — Irish farms had passed by millions of acres into native ownership.   The absentee, alien landlords with great estates that they seldom or never visited were doomed and fast vanishing and the way was being prepared — not without friction — for the small farmers and peasant proprietors who, today, defy the efforts of successive Irish republican Governments to put their country's agriculture on an internationally competitive footing.   This wholesale transfer of land was the first and most powerful factor in making the Ireland of 1912 peaceful.   But it was not the only one; the Irish were benefiting with their fellow citizens across St. George's Channel from the Old Age Pensions and other instalments of the Welfare State provided by Lloyd George.   And they were benefiting at British expense.

Until the turn of the century the national expenditure of Ireland had been less than her contribution to the common budget of the two islands.   By 1912 the balance had swung happily for her.   She was spending more than she herself raised and the deficit was coming out of John Bull's pocket.   As Asquith put it, in a typically rotund comment, the Irish enjoyed a 'copious flow of imperial doles'. He estimated that Irish revenue in 1912–13 would be £10,840,000 and expenditure on Irish services £12,350,000. Why then should Irishmen want to break away and to insist on the privilege of getting back their old Parliament on College Green or wherever it was and saddling themselves with debts which, if they kept quiet, their neighbours would pay for them? Their insistence was surely yet another example of how hopelessly deficient they had always been in common sense. This was a widespread reaction in Britain among men on both sides in politics and it was one that strengthened Conservative while weakening Liberal morale.

Conservatives, almost to a man, in and outside Parliament, regarded Home Rule as an absurd claim. Some brand of federalism, allowing Scotland and Wales along with Ireland to exercise glorified parish council powers, might conceivably be tolerated. There was talk of such a solution, but it can scarcely be said to have gone beyond the academic stage of discussion. Neither Scottish nor Welsh nationalism was yet organized and vocal enough to weigh with politicians anxious about votes. But to go further than a mild degree of federalism — how much further no one, not excluding the Government, was quite sure — and for Ireland alone would be folly. The British Empire must not show cracks in its structure to please a handful of Irish members who were amusing in their broguish way, but quite incompetent to run a country by themselves even with remote control from London. Left to themselves they might, at worst, try to cut completely adrift, and so imperil British security in war. Their ancestors had tried to do so in Napoleonic times and earlier under the Stuarts and the Tudors.

Even if that did not happen again in the twentieth century, Home Rule would mean Rome Rule and — however tolerant one might be in private and however polite one had to be in public about Roman Catholics — the fact remained that a country ruled by a majority of that religion was one in which a Protestant 'minority suffered. Was Britain to hand over loyal Protestants, North and South, to the tender mercies of their Pope-fearing compatriots? Belief was ineradicable in Protestant circles that Ireland was under the thumb of the Vatican — and the Noncomformist vote meant much to Asquith.

The Pope and his cardinals may well have received with wry smiles the news that the faithful in Ireland blindly obeyed orders from Rome. For the Irish had — and have — a secular habit of combining devotion to Catholicism with criticism of papal diplomacy and even, sometimes, of papal rulings. The early Christians in Ireland had so markedly refused to see eye to eye with their metropolitan governors on the date of Easter, the best way of shaving the heads of monks and other controversial matters, that the establishment of an heretical Celtic church was only with difficulty prevented. Since those far-off days, the rank and file of Irish Roman Catholics had continued occasionally to defy their bishops, when Nationalist emotions were running high, and had, more than once in their stormy history, sailed on a different course to that preferred by the Pope. Roman Catholics in Britain often found — and find — the behaviour of their Irish co-religionists embarrassing. Still, as every good British Nonconformist knew, they were, when all was said, priest-ridden, and the parish priest did — and does unquestionably — have more power over them than was enjoyed by any minister of religion in Britain.

Stimulus had been given, only a few months before, to these fears by a bitter debate in the House of Commons turning on the application of the papal decree, *Ne Temere*, to a mixed marriage in Belfast. A Presbyterian lady, a Mrs. McCann, was said to have had her children removed at the instigation of her Roman Catholic husband's priest. Birrell, the Chief Secretary, remarked in the course of this debate that a Presbyterian clergyman had thanked God for the McCann case because it showed the good people of England and Scotland what would happen if a Home Rule Ireland ever came into existence.

Gladstone himself had been unable, for all his hold on the Nonconformist conscience, to get round this difficulty. Looking back in old age on the dilemma of Liberalism, torn between respect for the rights of small nations and suspicion of Roman Catholic interference in politics and private life, Asquith sadly recalled how Dale, Spurgeon and other eminent Nonconformist clergy had deserted Gladstone and gone over to the Unionist camp. There was little danger of Victorian history repeating itself in 1912 to the extent of upsetting the Liberal hold on the House of Commons. Party feeling against the Tories was too fierce. But the raising again of the Irish question was bound to have a depressing effect on many thousands of Liberal voters.

Quite apart from the half-forgotten animosities, turning on religion and national safety, that were bound to be revived, there was universal reluctance to being taken again over the interminable rights and wrongs of Anglo-Irish history. Hibernian patriots were regarded as having only the saving grace of eloquence and wit in parliamentary debates to stop them from being crashing bores. Before you knew where you were when you got involved in an argument with them, they had led you back to Cromwell, and beyond him, into the mists of Brian Boru of whom you knew no more than that he was not, although his name suggested it, a Grand National winner. Like the Germans, the Irish had memories for every incident in their past and were inexhaustibly able and willing to remind — or rather to inform — you of occasion after occasion on which your ancestors had disgraced themselves in an island inhabited by a society of saints until the English made the crossing. Old political stagers, mindful of how often the Irish had forced them down that historical *via dolorosa* in the course of the Victorian Home Rule campaigns, shuddered at the prospect of having to tread it once more.

Thus from every point of view — except that of Parliamentary necessity — Home Rule was a cry that had better not have been heard arising from the Government benches. It is against this background that the personalities of the leading figures in this mounting conflict must now be seen.

CHAPTER II

WHO WAS WHO AND WHAT WAS WHAT

THE only member of Asquith's inner circle of Cabinet ministers with long and first-hand know-ledge of Ireland was John Morley, and he had been born as far back as 1838. When the Liberal Party split over Home Rule in the 'eighties, he had parted from his old radical ally Joseph Chamberlain, telling him, 'I have thought, read and written about Ireland all my life'. Gladstone twice made him Chief Secretary, an office that he held with loyalty to his leader and qualified success. He was accused of being too slow and cautious, but he had grappled manfully with the factious Irish groups and acquired in the process a close acquaintanceship with all the administrative difficulties of governing Ireland. His temperament and upbringing prevented him from ever acquiring that intuitive appreciation of changing mood and temper without which a ruler is lost in the treacherous climate of Irish affairs.

A product of early Victorian self-help, Morley had risen from humble north-country origins and graduated into politics through Oxford and the practice of sober journalism and authorship. He was a bookish man, charming in congenial society, fond of power and sometimes exasper-ating as a colleague. A prima-donnaish streak ran through him; Asquith was said to have more letters of resignation from him in the drawers of his desk than had ever before been sent by a minister. It was long since he had been directly concerned with Ireland. The monumental bio-graphy of Gladstone and the India Office had kept him occupied since just before the turn of the century.   He was listened to with respect as an elder statesman, but his counsel was of little use to Asquith on contemporary Ireland.

Asquith, too, had fought in the previous Home Rule campaigns.   His biographer and fellow Balliol man, J. A. Spender, claimed for him that 'he knew the Irish controversy by heart'.   But that was just what he did not know. His heart was not in the matter.   It was his brain that had, indeed, mastered every intricacy of the parliamentary twists and turns into which Gladstone led British politics on the Irish question.   He did not grasp that, when things were put to the final proof, the last word might not rest with Parliament.   He, like John Morley, was a perfect example of those Victorians who, being endowed with exceptional powers of passing the most difficult and competitive examinations, sincerely believed that to stick to one's books is the royal road to deserved success in life.

He was just old enough to remember the last phases of aristocratic privilege in affairs and of knock-about electioneering methods.   The purchase of commissions and of promotion in the army had been abolished in his youth. So had the hustings, the throwing of dead cats and rotten eggs and all the horse-play of the old Eatanswill sort of electioneering.   As a little boy walking to school, he had seen at Newgate corpses of a gang of five murderers swinging in public according to custom for an hour after their execution to impress passers-by.

Asquith as a statesman felt much as a doctor must have done who had lived through the era before anaesthetics into a less painful phase of surgery.   He was prepared for unlimited turbulence on the floor of the House — and well able to deal with it.   But it never seriously crossed his mind that a parliamentary issue might be fought out by unparliamentary means.   Compromise had hitherto saved the country from the revolutions that disturbed its neighbours.

Wellington had made the Tories bow to the pressure of public opinion over Reform and Peel had done the same over the Corn Laws. No political party in Britain ever had, or ever would defy the majority verdict of the Commons. The Home Rule Bill would, he recognized, be held up by the Lords for as long as they were now able to delay legislation of which they disapproved. But it could only be a limited delay, and the Bill would be an Act before 1914 was out. And that was all there was to the coming conflict.

Gladstone had told his wife that Home Rule was 'a debt owed by man to God'. Such a remark by Asquith to his wife Margot is unthinkable. He never soared to religious heights. His political convictions were based solidly on terra firma. So was the whole character of this massively reliable man. People in all camps trusted him, which was more than could be said of some of his colleagues. Few people trusted Lloyd George, and, at that date, Churchill was widely regarded as a brilliant, unreliable renegade from the Conservative Party. When the troubles were at their height, Asquith's solidity was to make him a tower of strength. He was respected by the Opposition and trusted by the high-ranking soldiers, who made in his case an exception to their general rule of not trusting politicians a yard. A popular song of a slightly later date recorded that 'Mr. Asquith said, in a voice very calm, "Another little drink won't do us any harm"'. This, as is the way of popular songs, expressed public opinion. The Prime Minister was held to be a sound North-country English-man, full of genial common sense as well as being an impressive lawyer.

The next two Liberal ministers to be reckoned with were of very different calibre. Lloyd George might have been expected to foresee the rough water ahead. He belonged to the Celtic fringe and he had shown himself in the Anglo-Boer War to be a courageous champion of small

peoples.   Had he been brought up in Tipperary instead of
in Caernarvonshire, he would certainly have been a leader,
if not the leader, of the Irish Party.   But, for some reason
that has never been explained, the sensitive antennae with
which Lloyd George explored so many dark and dangerous
avenues in the course of his long career were of little use
to him over Ireland.   He was to live gravely to misjudge
what was going on there when he was Prime Minister, and,
as Chancellor of the Exchequer in 1912, he gave no warning
to his learned chief of what was in store in the immediate
future.

But he shared with Churchill one prudent doubt that
was swept away by a majority decision of the Cabinet.
He and Churchill were in favour of excluding Ulster at the
outset from the operations of Home Rule.   That Churchill
should have been so was natural.   His filial piety, nurtured
on sincere family feeling and quickened by the sad fate of
his father, prompted him to take Lord Randolph Churchill
as his guide.   And Lord Randolph had been quick to see,
in the Gladstone days, that the slogan 'Ulster will fight
and Ulster will be right' was worth its weight in gold to
the Tories.   He had written to his friend, Lord Justice
FitzGibbon, 'I decided some time ago that, if the G.O.M.
went for Home Rule, the Orange card would be the one to
play.   Please God it may turn out the ace of trumps not
the two.'   His son, Winston, in 1912, was uneasily aware
that this commanding card was still in the hands of the
other side.

Churchill's earliest memories were of Ireland.   He had
lived, as a small boy, in the viceregal purple, his grandfather, the Duke of Marlborough, having been Lord-
Lieutenant and having appointed Lord Randolph as his
Secretary.   Churchill had learnt, in those impressionable
years, that Cromwell 'had blown up all sorts of things and
was, therefore, a very great man'.   He had been taught by
his nurse that the Fenians were wicked people, and on one

occasion, when he was riding on a donkey, a detachment of the Rifle Brigade out for a route march had been mistaken for Fenians. The alarm led to the donkey kicking and to Churchill getting concussion of the brain. 'This', he recorded afterwards, 'was my first introduction to Irish politics.'

Churchill would unquestionably have been temperamentally happier fighting against Home Rule side by side with his friend F. E. Smith and with Carson. He regarded the raising of the issue as a most disagreeable interference with the preparations in which he was absorbed for a possible world war. Since the issue was inescapable, he had sought from the beginning to keep it as little controversial as possible. 'From the earliest discussions on the Home Rule Bill in 1909', he has said, 'the Chancellor of the Exchequer and I had always advocated the exclusion of Ulster on a basis of county option or some similar process. We had been met by the baffling argument that such a concession might well be made as the final means of securing a settlement, but would be fruitless till then.'

Grey, the Foreign Secretary, had sided with Churchill and Lloyd George on the wisdom of including Ulster in this third Home Rule Bill, but his preoccupation with affairs in Europe had kept him from being an active partisan. This did not apply to the Lord Chancellor, Lord Loreburn, who brought the great weight of his authority down on the side of a whole-hogging Bill. He was to change his mind later and come out as an advocate of compromise, but, while the Cabinet was making up its mind, he helped to influence Asquith against what the majority of ministers decided would be premature concessions.

Loreburn, like Asquith, was a Balliol scholar. He had given remarkable proof, as an undergraduate, of his self-confidence in his own ability to triumph in examinations. Having won a demyship at Magdalen, he asked permission of the President to stand for Balliol without forfeiting his position in his own college. This impudent request was refused. Bob Reid, as he was then known, and as he was to continue to be known after he had been raised to the peerage, took a chance. He threw up his demyship and competed for and won his scholarship to Balliol. Unlike the Prime Minister, for whom a game of golf was a good walk spoiled, Loreburn had been a great athlete in his day, playing cricket for three years for Oxford. Awareness of effortless superiority was natural to such men. Looking across the House at the Opposition, strong though it was in dialectical ability, they felt that they could beat the ageing Balfour and the rest of them as they had repeatedly done in the past few years.

The present incumbent of the Irish Office was, like Morley, a mid-Victorian of Nonconformist stock, Augustine Birrell, the son of a Baptist minister in Liverpool. He had strayed from the narrow path of nonconformity, being lured away by the pleasures of being an accomplished *littérateur*. He was suspect in some Liberal quarters for being, in a literary way, too much a man of the world, just as Asquith was suspected of having been led by his second wife into a social world that had little in common with meat teas followed by speeches in favour of free trade.

Birrell was delightful company, and he was one of those Englishmen who appear, in each generation, generally on the left, with the conviction that they can get on with all kinds of foreigners by being tolerant towards their peculiar points of view. Birrell thoroughly enjoyed himself in the Dublin society which was then bubbling with the effervescence of the Gaelic Movement and the Abbey Theatre. He had no difficulty in getting on with the politicians of the Irish Nationalist Party. For all he understood of the troubles that were brewing under the surface in Ireland, he might as well never have crossed St. George's Channel.

Another member of the Cabinet to count in the coming

c

events was Haldane.   He, too, was a lawyer and his
intellectual equipment, based on a solid Scottish character,
had been tried in the fires of Hegelian philosophy.   At
this point he was Secretary of State for War, and the best
since Cardwell.   But the decisive calm and authority
with which he presided over general officers, who had, at
first, regarded him as an impossible highbrow and then
come both to respect and to like him, were shortly to be
disturbed.   Haldane, in a fateful moment for the Cabinet,
succeeded Loreburn as Lord Chancellor on June 10, 1912,
and was followed at the War Office by a very different
figure, Seely.

Haldane had happy memories of having enjoyed a
moment of triumphant diplomacy in Ireland.   He had
gone there in the days of the Balfour Government to
attempt to persuade the Roman Catholic hierarchy that
some proposed university reforms would not be dangerous
to the Church.   Hitherto, the Irish bishops had been
hostile and suspicious.   But Haldane won their confidence
as he was later to do that of the British generals.   He
described this remarkable feat in a letter to his mother to
whom he wrote regularly — he was a bachelor.

'Last night I cleared my last hurdle, and return having
accomplished what no Irish Secretary has ever succeeded
in doing, and what even Mr. Gladstone failed in.   The
Irish Hierarchy, the Nationalist Party and the Irish
Presbyterians, have been brought to agree on a scheme of
Irish University Education.

'I left Dublin in great secrecy with a warning from
Archbishop Walsh in my ears that I should probably fail
with Cardinal Logue.   I descended on him at night at
Armagh and lo ! in half an hour we had settled everything
in accordance with my scheme and were sitting down, he
in his Cardinal's red hat and I in a suit of dittoes, over two
dozen oysters (it is Friday) and a bottle of champagne.   If
the Government have any pluck, of which I am doubtful,

we ought to succeed now in solving this great problem. Healy and Dillon are much moved over my mission and I foresee a statue in Phoenix Park.'

But, unfortunately, Haldane had succeeded Loreburn as Lord Chancellor by the time the Home Rule troubles had reached their height. Had he remained at the War Office and not been followed by Seely, it is most improbable that the events to be described in this book would have happened.

The Marquis of Crewe, who held the India Office, had, in late Victorian times, been (as Lord Houghton) Lord-Lieutenant of Ireland while John Morley was Chief Secretary. But during the winter of 1911–12 he was in attendance on George V and Queen Mary on their Indian visit.

The Liberal ministry had, in making its decision, to take into account the pressure of its Nationalist allies in Parliament. They were not what they had been in the palmy days of Parnell. Their leader, John Redmond, came of an old Catholic southern family which had suffered much over the centuries for its faith. He had been chosen as leader, without much enthusiasm from his followers, to mend the split that had been left open for ten years after Parnell's fall. A decent man, he lacked the power of the partly American Parnell to keep discipline in that team of eloquent individualists. Discipline for the Irish Nationalists was harder to keep in 1912 than it had been a generation earlier. The collapse of Irish hopes in what Timothy Healy had called the stench of the divorce courts had left a bitterness that had by no means disappeared. The Irish were still liable to fight that old battle over again and some of them were able to persuade themselves that, somehow, it was Britain's fault that they had lost Parnell. The scandal caused in Irish Catholic circles no less than among English Nonconformists — to say nothing of less zealous men — by his relations with Mrs. O'Shea had, in fact, been enough to end his career. But it was argued that no scandal would have arisen had it not suited the book of those in Britain who were opposed to Home Rule to bring it out into the open. Joseph Chamberlain, now, in 1912, pathetically crippled and nearing his end, was privately regarded as the villain of the piece. But for him, Irish gossip asserted, Parnell might have kept his guilty secret from the public, as at least one Liberal minister near to Gladstone had done.

These retrospective recriminations did not make for party unity inside the Nationalist ranks and, although they were less acute than they had been at the turn of the century, they remained. Even if they had not, the Irish would have been less than a band of brothers. Healy and William O'Brien differed from John Dillon, and Redmond had his work cut out to keep his majority under control. 'There are two United Irish parties in this House', Healy once truthfully told the Commons, adding 'I am one of them.'

One bond was common to many of the leading Irishmen. They had been, in their youth, in dark Kilmainham gaol or one of its sister strongholds of the 'oppressor'. Redmond himself had been imprisoned. O'Brien, his claim to be treated as a political prisoner having been ignored, had refused to wear convict's uniform and had lain on his plank-bed for several weeks until, one morning, he was found clad in a suit of Blarney tweed which had been smuggled in by a warder. Both he and Dillon had escaped when out on bail, with the consent of their sureties, at a most inconvenient moment for the party; for, while they were still in exile and unable to return for fear of arrest, Parnell's divorce had been sprung on them.

The salad days of these now middle-aged men had thus been exciting. They had grown up amid the alarms and excursions of Fenianism and violent resistance to land-lordism. They were still to be reckoned with as orators in the Commons. One of them, Devlin, had been called

'Duodecimo Demosthenes' and, more affectionately — for most of these Irishmen were liked at Westminster — 'Wee Joe'. But they had not moved with the times. They were, as a whole, as is so common among revolutionaries who have grown mellow, an ineffective force hoping, for all their fiery speeches, that the promised land really was just round the corner for the Irish.

Had they been more in touch than they were with what was going on beneath the surface in Ireland, north and south, they would have been more help to Asquith. Southern Ireland was beginning to simmer with a nationalism that was to sweep the Nationalist Party off the board. Sinn Fein had already begun as a little-noticed movement. Redmond and his colleagues remained, in varying degrees, unaware of it as a potential source of future trouble. They disagreed among themselves on parliamentary tactics. Healy was expelled and readmitted and expelled again from the party. O'Brien founded an 'All for Ireland' League at variance with the orthodox Nationalists and having for its motto, 'Conference, Conciliation, Consent'; but neither he nor anyone else in the Irish parliamentary camp foresaw the full consequences of a British Government trying to force separation, however qualified, on the Protestant parts of Ulster.

It was the Conservative leaders who, from the start, sized up the realities of the situation and saw what a providential gift the Government was making to them. The Conservative leadership had passed, in the late winter of 1911, to Bonar Law. It had been an awkward passage. The party had, for some years previously, been disturbed by cries, growing more and more rude and loud, of 'Balfour must go'. But there had been a pretty evenly divided contest as to whether Walter Long or Austen Chamberlain should succeed him. Carson had been invited, and had refused to step into the breach which Bonar Law filled.

The new leader was a little-known and, to the general run of the party, an unimpressive Canadian business man. His full measure and the peculiar fitness of his character had not been realized. Asquith had described him as being 'meekly ambitious'. Bonar Law was a sound Conservative and, what was equally important, he was the son of a Presbyterian minister of Ulster farming stock. Conviction and background combined to throw him wholeheartedly into the Ulster crisis. He saw in it a means of bringing together the Conservative Party, of getting over the weakness of dissension inherited from Balfour's regime and of giving his followers something that they would really believe in fighting for. He might well, being the shrewd man he was, have seized on Ulster for tactical reasons even had he not felt strongly either way on the fundamental principles at stake. But he did feel strongly about them. It seemed to him monstrous that a Protestant section of the British people should be required to loosen, to however qualified an extent, their links with Westminster.

Bonar Law, left to himself, was not the man to set any heather on fire. He needed stimulus — and he got it from Carson. That southern Irishman, who became champion of the northern cause, saw, more quickly and more accurately than did any of his friends or foes, what could and could not be done in the unprecedented situation that was arising. He had, two years earlier, taken over the leadership of the Irish Unionists. Hitherto this had been, first, in the hands of Colonel Edward Saunderson and then in those of the no less gentle Walter Long. But, at the beginning of 1910, Long gave up his seat for South Dublin for one in London, and Carson took over.

At first the revolutionary nature of the change was not apparent. Carson had impressed himself on his contemporaries as a magnificent advocate and as the bonniest of legal fighters. His devastating cross-examination of

WHO WAS WHO AND WHAT WAS WHAT 21

Wilde had made him famous. He had beaten the proud
Lords of the Admiralty to their knees in a contest waged
with the gloves off, turning on the guilt or innocence
of the naval cadet, Archer-Shee, who has been given
posthumous dramatic life by Mr. Terence Rattigan in
The Winslow Boy. Carson had been Solicitor-General for
Ireland in the 'nineties, and, later, Solicitor-General for
England. But, until the difficulties over the succession of
the Conservative leadership arose, he had not made a
marked impression in the House. He was offered and
unhesitatingly refused the leadership of the Conservative
Party because his heart was always in Ireland. 'From the
day I first entered Parliament,' he said, 'devotion to the
Union has been the guiding star of my political life.'

He responded to the challenge of 1912 with grim delight.
He, like Bonar Law, saw what a boon it would be to
Conservative unity. His detestation of the whole idea of
separating the islands in any way was fierce. There were
those who said that Italian blood ran in his veins, and they
pointed to that saturnine, Dantesque profile as con-
firmatory proof. But his biographer, Colonel Montgomery
Hyde, has shown that there was nothing in the story.
The family were originally Scottish and Presbyterian.
Carson's grandfather had emigrated from Dumfries to
Dublin about the year of Waterloo. The origin of the
alleged Italian ancestry probably was that the grandfather
had kept a 'chip and straw warehouse' and specialized in
Leghorn and Tuscany hats. On his mother's side, Carson
came of Galway stock.

Born and brought up in Dublin, and practising as a
junior on the Leinster circuit, he had had little or no
dealings with Ulster until he came to lead its Protestants
into battle. His training in the Irish courts was an
invaluable background that gave him a grasp of the realities
which was completely beyond the range of other British
statesmen. His mind moved like that of an earlier Irish

statesman and lawyer, O'Connell, who had always gone on
the maxim that it is the verdict that counts. Men who
flourished in the Irish courts of Carson's day knew that
there was much more needed than law to win your case.
Juries had to be considered in ways alien to English
practice, and even judges, sometimes, gave an Hibernian
twist to the bench.

Carson knew instinctively what Irish emotion would
stand. His quick eye for the underlying facts of a case
detected that, given a lead, Protestant Ulster would follow
to any lengths of resistance. Every impulse prompted the
Ulstermen to hear Carson — and to obey. Positively,
they were loyal to the Crown and to every aspect of the
British connection. Negatively, they despised and dis-
trusted their Roman Catholic fellow-countrymen. Further
— and as important as anything else — they were in a
mood to live in exciting times as their fathers had done
before them and to escape for a while from the humdrum
everyday round of existence in this Fifth-Georgian period.

A shrewd observer, writing in the *Round Table* at the
time, remarked that 'modern Irish psychology, like certain
geological formations, is igneous in origin. Fierce streams
of lava and blinding showers of dust had been poured
upon the country out of a volcanic past.' Carson was
quite prepared to make the most of that volcanic past.
He knew his own mind. He did not know, in 1912, to
what extremities the policy of root-and-branch resistance
might lead — and he was not of the temperament to
worry once he had satisfied himself that ultimate victory
was certain. He had no doubt whatever but that, if Ulster
stood her ground — if she stood, should the necessity
arise, literally to her guns — the British Government,
whatever Acts of Parliament it might have got on to the
Statute Book, would be impotent.

Through the earlier stages of the resistance he was
laughed at by his Liberal critics as being a King of Bluffers.

In fact, he was an advocate of genius, self-confident, long before judge or jury had reached a decision, that he would gain a favourable verdict. He believed from the start that all the cards were in his hand. The British Conservatives, now that Bonar Law, and not Balfour, was leading them, would back him. The working out of details in a campaign was not his strong point, and these he left with well justified confidence to Captain Craig in Belfast. There was no better Ulsterman than Craig, who, luckily for the Orange cause, revealed a flair which amounted to genius for organizing mass meetings. Carson could not have asked for a better introduction to his new northern clients than he got from Craig when their campaign was first being warmed up in the autumn of 1911. Writing after the first of many historic meetings, Carson told Lady Londonderry that 'it was all magnificent, and Craig managed everything splendidly'.

Against this combination, traditional Liberal ways of thought, involving implicit trust in constitutional processes, were likely to be paralysed. Carson was encouraged to fight by Joseph Chamberlain, the old hero of resistance to Home Rule who was now crippled and nearing death, but still full of fire. Two new leaders of the resistance movement were to visit him at Highbury while the Home Rule struggle was at its fiercest, and he spoke to them almost identical words. To Carson, speaking with painful slowness, he said: 'If-I-were-you, I-would-fight-it-out-to-the-end', and to Mr. Amery, 'If-I-were-the-House-of-Lords, I-would-fight.' Constitutional processes only work if all parties affected by them, including minority parties, are prepared to play to the rules. Carson cared for the result, being sincerely convinced that justice was on his side, and did not give a fig for the rules. Herein his approach was the opposite to that of Asquith and completely acceptable to Ulster.

From time to time in history, songs are more relevant

than laws, and this was one such time. It would have
been well for the Cabinet had one of its members read
aloud, in the course of the troubled meetings held in the
winter of 1912, the words of 'The Old Orange Flute'.

> In the County Tyrone, in the town of Dungannon,
> Where many a ruction myself had a han' in,
> Bob Williamson lived, a weaver by trade,
> And all of us thought him a stout Orange blade.
> On the Twelfth of July as around it would come
> Bob played on the flute to the sound of the drum.
> You may talk of your harp, your piano or lute,
> But there's nothing compared with the ould Orange flute.
>
> But Bob the deceiver he took us all in,
> For he married a Papish called Brigid McGinn,
> Turned Papish himself, and forsook the old cause
> That gave us our freedom, religion, and laws.
> Now the boys of the place made some comment upon it,
> And Bob had to fly to the Province of Connacht.
> He fled with his wife and his fixings to boot,
> And along with the latter his old Orange flute.
>
> At the chapel on Sundays, to atone for past deeds,
> He said *Paters* and *Aves* and counted his beads,
> Till after some time, at the priest's own desire,
> He went with his old flute to play in the choir.
> He went with his old flute to play for the Mass,
> And the instrument shivered, and sighed: 'Oh, alas!'
> And blow as he would, though it made a great noise,
> The flute would play only 'The Protestant Boys'.
>
> Bob jumped, and he started, and got in a flutter,
> And threw his old flute in the blest Holy Water;
> He thought that his charm would bring some other sound,
> When he blew it again, it played 'Croppies lie down';
> And for all he could whistle, and finger, and blow,
> To play Papish music he found it no go;
> 'Kick the Pope,' 'The Boyne Water,' it freely would sound
> But one Papish squeak in it couldn't be found.
>
> At a council of priests that was held the next day,
> They decided to banish the old flute away,

For they couldn't knock heresy out of its head,
And they bought Bob a new one to play in its stead.
So the old flute was doomed and its fate was pathetic,
'Twas fastened and burned at the stake as heretic.
While the flames roared around it they heard a strange noise,
'Twas the old flute still whistling 'The Protestant Boys'.

This doggerel expressed a point of view that was to be inescapable in the coming months.   But it was not only religious animosity that still stirred the north; racial animosities, memories of siege and battle, divergences in economic ways of life kept Protestant Ulstermen and women apart from their neighbours in the south.   The gap was far wider than that dividing any two British political parties, and it would have been well for the Liberal Cabinet had all its members grasped and accepted this disagreeable but inescapable fact.

Ulster had stood out longer than had the other three provinces of Ireland (Leinster, Munster and Connaught) against British determination to destroy the old Celtic structure of society with its clan loyalties and complicated laws of land inheritance.   At the close of the first Elizabethan age, the Ulster chieftains still maintained a barbaric (as it seemed to the British) authority which had been taken away from most of their opposite numbers elsewhere in Ireland.   But, fearing that their days were numbered, they fled to Rome, and this 'Flight of the Earls', as it came to be called, left a highly convenient vacuum for James I to fill.   The native Irish were driven out of large tracts of Ulster, and Scottish and English settlers planted from Down and Antrim in the east to the city of Derry in the west, where to this day they remain.

Nothing comparable happened in the other provinces. Invaders had flowed in from Norman knights to Cromwellian troopers, but they had been absorbed, growing more Irish than the Irish themselves.   After a few generations Norman families came to be mixed up with the people

they had conquered and grandsons of the Ironsides who
had tossed Papist babies on pikes were speaking Irish
and attending Mass. An alien aristocracy owned great
estates as a legacy of these conquests, but nowhere, outside
Ulster, was there a solidly alien population. There the
settlers preserved and cherished alien characteristics; they
never forgot or lost pride in Scottish and English ancestry
and never ceased to keep on the alert, as a minority must
always do if it is to survive.

They kept the Protestant flag flying when William III
came over to settle conclusions with James II, and this
phase of history gave lasting inspiration to their feeling
of militant superiority to the rest of Ireland. They had,
it is true, bitter differences with their mother country,
detesting her episcopalian church and other aspects of
maternal interference. Many thousand Ulstermen emigrated to America in the eighteenth century. The
Declaration of Independence was set down in the handwriting of an Ulsterman. Washington declared 'if defeated everywhere I will make my last 'stand for liberty
among the Scotch-Irish of my native Virginia'. Fourteen
Presidents after Washington were of Ulster descent.
When, at the time of the French Revolution, England's
difficulty gave Ireland an opportunity to attempt to assert
herself, Ulstermen led the rebels. But they never threw
in their lot completely or merged with the older inhabitants
of Ireland.

As the nineteenth century wore on, this highly individual
section of the Irish population drew away for new reasons
from its neighbours. Ulster shared with Britain in the
changes brought about by the industrial revolution which
passed the rest of Ireland by. The shipyards and the
linen mills made Ulster conscious of world markets and of
sharing a common outlook with British industrialists.
Belfast business men travelled in the Dominions and in
foreign parts, extending the prosperity of their native city.

IRELAND

The six counties of Ulster now forming Northern Ireland }

The three counties of Ulster now in the Republic of Ireland }

SCOTLAND

Lamlash 7 miles

ANTRIM

Londonderry
LONDON-
DERRY

Larne

Copeland 1½°

DONEGAL

Ballymena

Holywood

TYRONE

Belfast

Lisburn

Bangor

Donaghadee

Sligo

FERMANAGH

ARMAGH

DOWN

MONAGHAN

CAVAN

R E P U B L I C

R. Boyne

Dublin

Howth

Athlone

R. Shannon

Kingsbridge

Kingstown
(Dun Laoghaire)

Galway

Kildare

Newbridge

Curragh

O F

I R E L A N D

Limerick

Waterford

Cork

Scale of Miles

50

100

The rest of Ireland stagnated economically and was described with truth, though with the licence of caricature, by Bernard Shaw in *John Bull's Other Island*.

There was no more hope of Edwardian Ulster peacefully accepting Home Rule than there was of Leinster, Munster and Connaught being happy until they got it. The dilemma of any British Government was how to reconcile these two conflicting views without coming to blows with one or other party or with both and — no less important — without the two parties coming to blows between themselves. The Liberal Government, in choosing to treat the Irish problem as purely one of Westminster politics, had behind them a series of unhappy precedents. Successive British ministers had burnt their fingers through not taking a contemporary line on Ireland. It was such a protean place to grasp ; its mood, at least on the surface, was always changing. Disraeli had expressed this well in his flippant way when he had said it was the Pope one day and potatoes the next. He never visited Ireland, and Gladstone only once did so, and then for little more than three weeks largely spent in great houses.

Both these Victorian Prime Ministers had shared one hope which may or may not have been an illusion. They would have liked the Prince of Wales to have lived in Ireland so that capital might have been made out of the reverence for royalty with which the Irish were alleged to have been endowed. Disraeli had drawn a tempting picture for the Queen of a suitable residence in an Irish hunting country where the Prince might 'combine the fulfilment of public duties with pastime, a combination which befits a princely life'. The Queen's reaction had been immediate and emphatic. Such a notion was 'not to be thought of', 'quite out of the question' and 'could never be considered'.

Gladstone made similar proposals and was similarly rebuffed. Ireland, he was told by the Queen, was not on the same plane as Scotland as far as a royal residence was concerned. The mild controversy went on until nearly the end of the old lady's reign, but Edward had to be content with several visits in the course of which there was trouble with his mother, caused by what she regarded as his excessive fondness for race-courses, a taste that had led to the inclusion of the Punchestown meeting in his itinerary. Had a Balmoral or a Sandringham been established in Ireland, the Irish as a whole would have been delighted to welcome a Prince among them. But there would unquestionably have been the danger, up to the end of the nineteenth century, of some fanatics trying to murder him. Such possibilities of violence seemed to have faded almost to the point of invisibility by the time the Liberals came into office. So tranquil was the scene that Asquith, like most of his party followers, thought that no more than a political settlement had now to be effected. That Ulster was to prove as intractable as all the other three provinces put together had been in the past did not come into his calculations.

A fatal stress was laid by the politicians on the fact that all Ulster was not against Home Rule. Three of its counties, Monaghan, Donegal and Cavan, had large Nationalist and, so, Home Rule majorities. Two others, Fermanagh and Tyrone, were evenly balanced with a slight bias in favour of the Nationalists. This reduced the indigestible Orange core to at the most Antrim, Armagh, Down and Derry, and even there strong Nationalist pockets existed. There was, thus, some excuse for dismissing the Ulster bogy, but not much; for anyone who had troubled to get to know the north and to understand the depth and fervency of its imperialism, of its Protestantism and of its deep-seated suspicion of the Catholic south, would not have been deceived.

CHAPTER III

PREPARING TO MEET PARLIAMENT

T HE month of January 1912, through part of which
Asquith relaxed in Sicily, was not an idle one for
the Ulstermen. On the 5th they took a remarkable
step forward in their preparations for defying the constitution. Response to the invitation to do so had been
gratifying to Carson and Craig; the rank-and-file of both
sexes had shown itself eager to volunteer. It was plain
that able-bodied Protestants of military age were prepared
to drill and that their women-folk, led by Lady Londonderry
and other great ladies, would work as though a war were
round the corner.

But, in fact, it was a time of peace and the leaders, who
left nothing to chance, did not want to find that the
enthusiasm they were whipping up stood in danger of a
cold douche from the law. So, on January 5, they applied
to the Belfast justices for leave to drill the Orange Lodges.
Colonel Wallace, one of the members of the Provisional
Executive of the Ulster 'Government' which was being
brought into being, was a solicitor who had commanded a
battalion of the Royal Irish Rifles in the Anglo-Boer war.
He applied to the courts 'for lawful authority to hold
meetings . . . for the purpose of training and drilling
and of being trained and drilled to the use of arms and for
the purpose of practising military exercises, movements
and evolutions'. The reason why this unusual permission
was sought was nicely put. The Lodges, it stated, 'desire
this authority as faithful subjects of His Majesty the King
only to make them more efficient citizens for the purpose

of maintaining the constitution of the United Kingdom as now established and protecting their rights and liberties thereunder'.

The local magistrates granted the necessary permission and, as the winter months dragged on and the date of the introduction of the Home Rule Bill approached, open drilling became more and more active. The volunteers had, at this stage, one disadvantage. They were not adequately equipped with arms and were forced to drill with dummy rifles. But, as one of the earliest acts of the Liberal Government on coming into power had been to abolish the long-standing prohibition on the import of guns into Ireland, this lack was regarded by Ulster as merely temporary. Meanwhile, it allowed British Liberal critics to cheer themselves up by laughing at this playboy force wasting its time sloping arms with wooden toys.

Statesmen on both sides of the water went oratorically into action with the volunteers. On the day after the obliging magistrates had legalized Carson's army, Balfour, in Scotland, denounced the Government for its 'abominable' behaviour in having tricked citizens at the last General Election by alleging that Home Rule was not the issue before them. This was an argument of which more was to be heard through the ensuing debates in and outside Parliament. The Conservatives made much of the point that the Government had no right to force a Home Rule Bill through without first going to the country. Against this, the Liberals protested that every elector in 1910 and in 1906 had been perfectly well aware that Home Rule was a traditional plank of Liberal policy. Both sides ransacked the election addresses and speeches of their opponents.

The truth behind this interminably wordy warfare lay obviously between the two extreme cases. No one had ever supposed that the Liberals would not sooner or later have to introduce a measure of Home Rule, and, at the

D

same time, the issue had not been given prominence at any one of the three General Elections won by the Liberals in the past six years. How far a Government is entitled to put forward far-reaching and controversial legislation without having first made it the main plank in a campaign or the subject of a plebiscite is always arguable.

Carson followed up Balfour by declaring that he was a rebel in the sense that he wished to remain under the King and the Imperial Parliament, and he said, somewhat cryptically, that he would regard the opening of an Irish Parliament by the King as an insult.

The noise of these opening shots in the campaign was drowned by the roar of hostility that greeted the announcement of Churchill's intention to speak in favour of Home Rule at the Ulster Hall in Belfast, that is, in the holy of holies of Orangemen. Tempers were already quickening when this provocative arrangement was made public. The Liberal *Daily News* informed its outraged readers that a leaflet had been circulated at an Orange meeting calling on Germany, as the great Protestant power, to come and save Ulster from being ruled by the Pope. Churchill's intention was denounced in Belfast as showing a willingness to dance on his father's coffin.

It was decided that Churchill must be kept out of the Ulster Hall. On a motion of Craig, the Standing Committee of the Ulster Unionist Council observed 'with astonishment the deliberate challenge thrown down by Mr. Winston Churchill, Mr. John Redmond, Mr. Joseph Devlin and Lord Pirrie in announcing their intention to hold a Home Rule meeting in the centre of the loyal City of Belfast, and resolves to take steps to prevent its being held'. The presence of Lord Pirrie as chairman was taken as adding insult to injury, for, as a special correspondent of *The Times* wrote, 'Lord Pirrie deserted Unionism about the time the Liberals acceded to power and soon afterwards was made a peer; whether *propter*

hoc or only *post hoc* I am quite unable to say — though no
Ulster Unionist has any doubts on the subject'.

Churchill was not the man to bow to threats, but in
common sense he had to think again about the wisdom of
this trailing of his coat. Lord Riddell, calling on him early
in February, found him dressing, and noted in his diary,
'He spoke vehemently regarding his visit to Belfast,
pointing his observations with his safety-razor. He said
that the forthcoming session was likely to be one of the
most violent on record. He referred bitterly to Sir Edward
Carson and said he had been stirring up trouble.' But,
recognizing that the trouble had been stirred efficiently,
Churchill offered to hold his meeting elsewhere, and this
offer was accepted. Still, the presence of a Liberal member
who, because of his father, was regarded as a renegade,
might well lead to trouble.

While Government supporters protested against this
infringement of the rights of free speech in the Ulster
Hall, the authorities in Belfast made anxious preparations
to ensure that the meeting in another place went off
quietly. The place chosen was the football ground of the
Celtic Park, a Catholic club. Lord Edward Gleichen, a
Grenadier who commanded an infantry brigade in Belfast,
felt himself saddled with the distasteful task of having
responsibility for helping to keep law and order.

'Finding myself about the only person in some
authority with no axe to grind,' he wrote, 'I communicated
with the Roman Catholic Bishop, Tohil, a man of some
character, with the Liberal Association, with one or two
Nationalists, Lord Londonderry and Colonel Wallace
(Grand Master of the Orangemen) — all with a view to
getting them to restrain their different flocks from making
disturbances on the day. From all these, except the
Unionists, I got assurances that they would do their best.
I was much disconcerted at receiving a polite note from
Lord Londonderry (with whom I had been shooting at

Mount Stuart only a month before), saying that he regretted he could not meet me on the matter. I caught, however, Colonel Wallace, but he would promise nothing. At last he said that if I would guarantee the presence of a large number of troops, he would see what he could do. I guaranteed him 3,500, but he did not move until they arrived. Then he got to work. There was more method in this than I suspected at the time. The fact was that the Unionist chiefs refused to give any guarantee or promise for this reason, that they thought that if Dublin Castle were to hear that the Orangemen had promised to keep order they (the Castle) would countermand the troops coming and would throw the whole blame of any disturbance that might occur onto the Orangemen. Hence they waited.'

The troops duly arrived — four battalions of infantry and a squadron of cavalry in Victoria Barracks and three battalions at Holywood. Part of this force was stationed, on the day, at Celtic Park and the rest was kept, in Gleichen's words, 'lying doggo at different points in the town'.

Churchill was received at the quay at Stranraer by crowds hooting him and his wife and singing 'Rule Britannia' and the national anthem. The visitors smiled and entered a saloon carriage with blinds drawn. Another crowd awaited him at Belfast, grinning when he raised his hat. Youths waving flags and brandishing stout sticks surrounded his hotel. A black effigy, intended to represent the visitor, was burnt in the forefront of the procession. So thick were the surging crowds around the car that took him to the ground that it was momentarily poised on its near-side wheels and might have been overturned. A correspondent, following in a press car, reported that men thrust their heads in and 'uttered fearful menaces and imprecations'.

The scene changed when the Falls — the Catholic

quarter — was reached.   There effigies of Londonderry and Carson were to be seen hanging in contrast to those of Redmond and Churchill displayed in the Protestant quarter of Shankhill Road.   Churchill was allowed to make his fighting speech, though it was interrupted in a manner quite unconnected with Ireland and with which he and all Liberal ministers were only too familiar.   A woman shouted, in a broad Ulster accent, 'Will you give the suffrage to women ?'   After the meeting, and on police advice, the return journey was taken by back streets. Responsible men on all sides breathed a sigh of relief when his ship sailed from Larne.   And to this the Orangemen triumphantly added the reflection that Lord Randolph Churchill had been welcomed like a king, while his son had slunk away like a thief in the night.

Agitation in Britain against Home Rule was now growing.   The Irish Presbyterians had appealed to the English Nonconformists, one of whose ministers in Hampstead, the Reverend Robert Horton, well expressed the dilemma of this important section of Liberalism.   He regarded Home Rule, he declared, as an act of political justice, but he hoped that a remedy might be found in the emigration to Great Britain of Irish Protestants and to Ireland of English Roman Catholics.   It was a beautiful and simple thought — too beautiful and simple to come true.

The Cabinet, unable to take refuge in the optimism of the Reverend Robert Horton, spent February in anxious debate on whether Ulster, or at least its Protestant counties, should be allowed to contract out of the Bill that was shortly to be introduced, or whether this relief should be kept as a later tactical concession.   They decided on one of those carefully drafted compromises which are more attractive to legal minds than effective under the conditions of rough justice that prevail in politics.   Asquith, in a Cabinet letter to the King on February 6, wrote that 'the Government hold themselves free to make changes, if it became clear that special treatment must be provided for the Ulster counties, and that in this case the Government will be ready to recognize the necessity either by amending or by not pressing it (the Bill) on under the provision of the Parliament Act'.

The plain meaning of this was that the Government, in spite of the warning signals that were coming over from Northern Ireland, felt confident that Parliament would have the last word. There would be rows in the House in response to which concessions would be made, more especially concessions over using the recently granted power of steam-rollering the Lords. Ulster would, in some way, be excluded if parliamentary resistance to her being kept inside the framework of Home Rule proved too strong. But, as Asquith's biographer put it, 'no sober-minded Englishman' at this point supposed that the arming and drilling would amount to effective resistance to the will of Parliament, or that, however flamboyantly Ulstermen might stand up on their hind legs, 'in so doing they would be supported and encouraged by one of the great English parties'.

No less confident was the conviction that soldiers must not reason why. The possibilities of their doing so had arisen in the course of the grim coal strike that was then agitating the country more than was the stage army marching about in Ulster. At the Central Criminal Court in March, Guy Bowman, Editor of the *Syndicalist*, and the printers of that journal were sentenced respectively to five months and to six months imprisonment for publishing an article inciting soldiers to disobey any order to fire on strikers.

The article, strong stuff, had been entitled 'Open Letter to British Soldiers'. It began 'Men, Comrades, Brothers — You are in the army, so are we — you in the army of destruction, we in the industrial, or army of construction. We work at mine, mill, forge, factory or dock, etc., producing and transporting all the goods, clothing stuffs etc. which make it possible for people to live; you are working men's sons. When we go on strike to better our lot, which is the lot also of your fathers, mothers, brothers and sisters, you are called upon by your officers to murder us. Don't do it. You know how it happens — always has happened. We stand out as long as we can. Then one of our (of your) irresponsible brothers, goaded by the sight and thought of his loved ones' misery and hunger, commits a crime on property. Immediately you are ordered to murder us as you did at Mitchelstown, at Featherstone, at Belfast. Don't you know that when you are out of the Colours and become a civilian again that you, like us, may be on strike, and you, like us, be liable to be murdered by other soldiers? Boys, don't do it. "Thou shalt not kill" says the Book. Don't forget that. It doesn't say — "unless you have a uniform on". No; murder is murder, whether committed in the heat of anger on one who has wronged a loved one or by pipe-clayed Tommies with rifles.'

The jury, after a short absence, had found the defendants guilty, and Mr. Justice Horridge said, in giving his verdict, that he was going to let the offenders off lightly because there had not been a prosecution for such an offence for a great many years. As his verdict was being delivered, a voice at the back of the court called out 'Liar', and after the learned judge had passed sentence a man exclaimed, 'It is our turn next', and several persons were ejected by the police.

Tom Mann was, in the same week, prosecuted in the Salford Police Court under the 'Incitement to Mutiny Act', the charge being based on the *Syndicalist* article and on two speeches that this fiery left-winger had recently made at meetings of the Workers' Union, an advanced Labour organization of which he was leader. Mann had prophetically remarked after one of those meetings: 'You must not be surprised if I am arrested and find myself in court'.

The proceedings were interesting because of the remarks made by Gordon Hewart (famous as Lord Chief Justice in the nineteen-thirties for his robust assertion of the virtues of corporal punishment) on behalf of the Director of Public Prosecutions. Hewart, basing his case on the Incitement to Mutiny Act of 1797, argued that a soldier has a twofold capacity. Lord Mansfield had said that a soldier is bound 'to all the duties of other citizens and he is bound to prevent a felony or breach of the peace as any other citizen. More than that, if it be necessary for the prevention of mischief or for the execution of law, it is not only the right but the duty of soldiers to exert themselves in assisting the execution of legal processes and to prevent commission of crime or mischief.' Hewart also quoted the dictum of Lord Chief Justice Tyndal that 'where danger is present or immediate, the military subjects of the King not only may but must do their utmost to prevent the perpetration of an outrage, to put down riot and tumult and to preserve the lives and property of the people.'

Mann, in the speeches that had brought him into court, had said, among other things, that he would always be one to tell soldiers not to shoot their comrade workers but to 'turn your rifles round and shoot the other people'. He was not to be intimidated into silence, for 'By all the gods and devils, I'll teach the Government. I'll not stand it.' He had in mind, when he spoke thus boldly, strikers in Wales and Liverpool rather than volunteers in Ulster, but the echo of his sentiments was soon to be heard in an Irish context. Meanwhile, he was sentenced to six months imprisonment in the second division, and was released after less than seven weeks. Spender's 'sober-minded Englishmen' were shocked but not alarmed by Mann's wild words. A spell, but not too long a one, of cooling his heels in gaol would meet the case.

All this was in the minds of members when the House
of Commons reassembled at the beginning of April and,
in the course of disposing of the Army (Annual) Bill,
Keir Hardie, another of the wild men, moved an amendment. It would have given recruits the option of refusing
beforehand to assist the civil power in a trade dispute.
This, in spite of the support it gained from Lansbury and
Wedgwood, was regarded by the War Minister as 'fantastic'
and was defeated by 168 to 23. On the third reading, the
Attorney-General explained that the general principle
was that the soldier could be called on for the prevention
or in anticipation of a riot or of some attack on life or
on the community. It would depend on circumstances
whether soldiers could be put to drive trams or otherwise
to take the place of strikers. The House was not particu-
larly interested in these exchanges; all its thoughts were
concentrated on the introduction by the Prime Minister
on the next day of the Bill 'to Amend the Provision for the
Government of Ireland'.

This was on Thursday April 11, and, with a nice sense
of timing, the Ulstermen got in ahead over the previous
week-end, which was Easter, with a series of bigger and
better demonstrations. They were followed with approval
by many observers in England. Excitement was in the
spring air on both sides of St. George's Channel. A
member of the Carlton Club proposed, in the suggestion
book, that 'the Union Jack should be kept flying on the roof
until the Home Rule Bill were defeated or withdrawn'.

CHAPTER IV

THE DRILLING BEGINS

THE dramatic feature that made Easter of 1912 so memorable in Ulster was that Bonar Law, accompanied by some seventy members of Parliament from English, Scottish and Welsh constituencies, was present, and they all let themselves go. It was a transformation scene in contrast to that in which Churchill had been the principal actor. One hundred thousand men marched in military formation past a saluting-point where Bonar Law stood. Lord Hamilton at the head of the Prentice Boys of Derry led them and, a reporter noted, 'throughout one saw mingled in the ranks patrician and plebeian, clergy and laity, masters and men — that effacement of class distinction that is significant of the movement in the truest sense national'. He also noticed with approval that it was 'a remarkably well dressed crowd, the Belfast shipwrights looking especially well turned out'.

Seventy special trains had brought the demonstrators to Belfast. Gleichen and his troops were not needed, and hardly a policeman was visible. Even the weather appeared to have taken on an orange tinge. It had rained hard for poor Churchill; now it was fine.

On the main platform the proceedings were opened with prayer by the Primate of All Ireland and the whole vast gathering sang the Ninetieth Psalm. Carson led off the speeches with what was now becoming his ominous gramophone record — 'We will never in any circumstances submit to Home Rule'. Bonar Law followed, assuring his hearers that though the brunt of the battle would be theirs, they would not be wanting help from across the Channel. Inspired by the atmosphere to flights of oratory to which he did not normally aspire to mount, he asked himself how radical Scotsmen would like to be treated as the Government was treating Protestant Ulster, and, answering himself, he replied, 'I know Scotland well, and I believe that rather than submit to such a fate, the Scottish people would face a second Bannockburn or a second Flodden'.

The planners did not confine themselves at these meetings to seeing that the oratory was worthy of the occasion. Their stage management left nothing to chance. Bonar Law, Carson, Londonderry and others took a salute with a Union Jack measuring 48 ft. by 25 ft., said to be the largest ever woven, breaking above them from a signalling tower as a resolution against Home Rule was put and riotously carried. Bonar Law encouraged his hearers not to be depressed by the size of the ministerial majority now cemented, as he unkindly reminded them, through the new payment of members 'by £400 a year'. The Government, by the Parliament Act, had erected a boom against them, to shut them off from the help of the British people. But they would burst that boom as their fathers had done in the famous old days at Derry.

Commentators in Britain who sympathized with Ulster began, at this point, to be openly uneasy. *The Times* observed that 'the Gracchi of the Liberal — and of the Nationalist — parties will doubtless see much to reprehend in the attitude of those who gathered in defence of their civil and religious liberties yesterday'. But the writer went on to encourage himself by pointing out that 'the Ulstermen and their leaders are quite prepared for that. They do not admit the right of Parliament — and still less of Parliament as the Liberals have maimed it — to deprive them of their fundamental rights as British citizens. They agree with Mr. Bonar Law that, in all history, no precedent exists for such a step. They will not have one created at their expense. . . . It would take them from under the protection of the British Government and of the British Parliament to place them under the rule of men whose ways are not as their ways and whose standards are not their standards — under the men who control the United Irish League and the Ancient Order of Hibernians. To them that rule means ruin. They will not submit to it, unless it is forced upon them by arms, and they cannot bring themselves to believe that their British fellow subjects will consent to force it upon them.'

Spender's *Westminster Gazette*, the London evening paper which was closest to Asquith, struck a gayer note. Its cartoonist, F. C. Gould, drew a costermonger's donkey-cart in which Carson, Londonderry and Bonar Law, refreshed by 'Orangeade', took 'an Easter jaunt in Ulster'. Kipling, in the *Morning Post*, the most hard-hitting of the Tory papers, lashed out in the other direction.

> The dark eleventh hour
> Draws on and sees us sold
> To every evil power
> We fought against of old.
> Rebellion, rapine, hate,
> Oppression, wrong and greed
> Are loosed to rule our fate,
> By England's act and deed.
>
> The faith in which we stand,
> The laws we made and guard,
> Our honour, lives, and land
> Are given for reward
> To Murder done by night,
> To Treason taught by day,
> To folly, sloth, and spite,
> And we are thrust away.
>
> The blood our fathers spilt,
> Our love, our toils, our pains,
> Are counted us for guilt,
> And only bind our chains.

Before an Empire's eyes,
The traitor claims his price.
What need of further lies?
We are the sacrifice.

We know the war prepared
On every peaceful home,
We know the hells declared
For such as serve not Rome —
The terror, threats, and dread
In market, hearth, and field —
We know, when all is said,
We perish if we yield.

Believe, we dare not boast,
Believe, we do not fear —
We stand to pay the cost
In all that men hold dear.
What answer from the North?
One Law, one Land, one Throne.
If England drive us forth
We shall not fall alone.

It was with such conflicting previews before them that members settled down to hear what the long-heralded Bill contained.

Ringing cheers from the Opposition greeted Bonar Law as he entered the House with the laurels of his Ulster tour on him, and the Prime Minister, as he spoke with great deliberation from carefully prepared notes, was repeatedly interrupted by ironical applause. Spender has called the Bill 'one of the might-have-beens' of British history. Emphasis was laid in it on the federalist idea, because the Government vainly hoped that this might placate the academic federalists of the Conservative Party. Asquith pointed out that there were already between twenty and thirty self-governing legislatures under the allegiance of the Crown. What would be more sensible than still further to relieve the pressure of congestion at Westminster by having a single Imperial Parliament there and giving, in due course, to Scotland, Wales and even England, what was now being offered to Ireland. This was derisively rejected as being an absurd attempt to 'restore the Heptarchy' — the division of England into little kingdoms in Saxon times.

The defence shifted. No one need fear that sovereignty of the Imperial Parliament would be weakened in essentials. It would continue to control foreign affairs, the army and navy, peace and war and taxation. It would have the power to allow or to repeal any act of the Irish Parliament. Irish members would continue to come to Westminster but in mercifully reduced numbers, being cut down to 42. There would be no danger of discriminatory religious legislation getting passed in Dublin, because the Parliament there was to be prevented from making laws either directly or indirectly to the advantage of any church.

What all this amounted to was the setting up of local government with limited authority, very much on the lines that prevail today in the six counties of Northern Ireland. The Act of 1920 which established the present Parliament in Northern Ireland reproduced textually the main provisions of the Bill of 1912. It is proof of how swiftly the Nationalist sentiment was to be inflamed in the next few years that this cautious and severely qualified measure should have seemed outrageous to so many people in 1912 but in 1920 appear no more than a harmless, necessary concession.

To Redmond, it seemed, after he had heard the debate, like a dream coming true. 'If I may say so reverently,' he told the House, 'I personally thank God that I have lived to see this day.' But that was far from being the sentiment of the House. Asquith and Bonar Law indulged in some sharp exchanges. The Prime Minister reproached the Leader of the Opposition for having said at Belfast that the Government had sold the constitution and themselves. That, he commented reprovingly, was 'the new style'. He asked whether Bonar Law would repeat in the House that ministers were selling their convictions. 'You have not got any,' said Bonar Law. 'We get on with the new style,' said Asquith.

Prominent men in the Dominions and in the United States, including the Mayor of New York and several state governors, telegraphed their approval of this belated instalment of justice to Ireland, and continental opinion was, on the whole, favourable. The House was unmoved by these reactions from overseas as it went on to dissect the Bill clause by clause. The *Titanic* went down while the debate was at its height, giving scope for the use, from the Conservative benches, of some grim maritime metaphors. Eloquence was the order of the day. Lord Hugh Cecil declared that the Bill reduced Ireland from the status of wife to that of mistress. Unionists claimed that they looked on the proposed transfer with at least as much horror as Poland looked on her transfer to Russia. The eventuality of troops being used came up. Would the Prime Minister give orders to shoot down men whose only claim was that they refused to be driven out of the community? For the first, but by no means the last, time in the weary progress of the Bill, the closure was applied, leave to introduce being granted amid stormy scenes by 360 to 266.

On the same day, the Irish Church synod issued a protest against it which was not quite unanimous, for there were five dissentients, including the Rev. J. O. Hannay, better known as the novelist George A. Birmingham. At the second reading, Churchill begged members to bring a 'modern eye' to bear and, giving his private misgivings an airing, he admitted that apprehension in parts of Ulster was genuine and should not be treated contemptuously. But what did Ulster want? It could not impose a permanent veto. It had duties as well as rights, a great sacrifice and a great opportunity was before the Ulstermen, and if they refused, Churchill ended, somewhat menacingly, they would not be allowed to obstruct the work of salvage.

Whitsun saw the beginning of the committee stage, and the moving, by Agar-Robartes, a Liberal member for a Cornish constituency, of an amendment excluding from the Bill the counties of Antrim, Armagh, Down and London-derry. 'Orange bitters and Irish whiskey will not mix', he warned the House. Throughout the summer the wrangle went on. The use of the closure was denounced as intolerable insolence and bullying tactics.

Feelings were inflamed by an attack on a Sunday School procession at Castledawson in County Londonderry. An Orange member asked the Chief Secretary for Ireland why Nationalists had assaulted some harmless Protestant school children. Before Birrell could reply, a Nationalist member from Mayo asked why a large number of Orange-men had armed themselves with 'quantities of stones' and gone into the attack with cries of 'To hell with the Pope.' Birrell did his best to disentangle these conflicting sugges-tions. A Sunday School excursion party of about 500, many of them women and children, and accompanied by a band, had met four bands belonging to the Ancient Order of Hibernians, some 300 strong. The police had done their best to supervise the passing of the two crowds, but one of the Hibernians had dashed into the excursion party and a general row at once ensued. The excursionists were reinforced by Protestants from the town. Stones were thrown by both sides. A blue banner, which was being carried by the excursionists, was pulled away from them, but was rescued by the police and restored to its owners.

This was not good enough for Dillon, who wanted a full enquiry. Birrell stuck to his point that it had been more than a matter of women and children. In the fight, one of the Royal Irish Constabulary, a brave and active man, had been violently kicked in the stomach. 'By a

THE VOLUNTEERS PREPARE FOR ACTION

Hibernian ?' asked Craig. 'I do not suggest it was done by a child,' Birrell answered.

Whichever side may have been the aggressor at Castle-dawson, the affair clearly called for reprisals, and with little delay they came. The co-religionists of the Protestant children were in the majority in the shipyards of Belfast where they had, handy and in plentiful supply, those iron nuts and rivets which are known as Belfast confetti. Confetti was freely thrown in July. Catholics were driven out of employment by threats from their Protestant fellow workers and prudently would not go back until their safety was assured. Protestant youths chased Catholic men into the dock. One swam for safety, took refuge in a workshop where the foreman, who tried to protect him, was knocked down and kicked.

Craig blamed Catholic militancy at Castledawson for these rough-houses. Birrell did not agree, believing that such a view was a complete delusion. What remained certain was that an appetite for violence was growing in Ulster to an extent that gave some alarm to the responsible leaders of the resistance movement. They prepared to deflect the pugnacity of their following into controlled channels. But before they acted the Prime Minister had taken a bold step. He went to Ireland — the first British Prime Minister in history to do so.

Kingstown, now called Dun Laoghaire (and pronounced Dun Leary), was gay with bunting when he arrived, and it was remarked that if he thought the flags were in his honour, no great harm was done, although they were in fact being flown in honour of the local regatta. But the reception in Dublin was more mixed. As Asquith and his wife and daughter, accompanied by Redmond, were driven past the General Post Office, a woman threw a hatchet, which missed the Prime Minister and inflicted a small wound, which drew blood slightly, on Redmond's ear. This reminder that women, determined to have the vote,

E

were no less militant than Ulster people determined not to have Home Rule, was followed up more spectacularly in the course of the evening.

Asquith spoke then at the Theatre Royal before a packed house, the audience in which had been rigorously scrutinized, for each ticket had been examined at least twice. 'All the arrangements,' it was reported, 'were indeed of Russian severity.' But this had not prevented several ladies, visitors from Britain, from having got into the theatre with gunpowder and paraffin oil and having made a too nearly successful attempt to burn the place down. Happily this was prevented by the prompt action of Sergeant Cooper of the Connaught Rangers and Colour-Sergeant Shea of the Royal Welch Fusiliers. One lady had saturated the carpet of the dress circle with oil and then set fire to it. The soldiers succeeded, with difficulty, in beating out the flames with their coats.

Sergeant Cooper said in evidence that as he and his friend, Colour-Sergeant Shea, both stationed at the Curragh, and their wives were leaving the theatre, they noticed that the carpet was alight and that there was a lot of fluid on it, like petrol or oil. He saw a lady striking a match to set more fire to it. He and the Colour-Sergeant pulled off their overcoats and managed to put the fire out, and then there was an explosion, which he described in the witness-box as being 'like a report from a cannon, and there was smoke like that following the discharge of a field artillery gun. The place was all cloudy.' He had seen one of the accused running upstairs, and had followed her and caught hold of her, and both of them had fallen down the stairs. He was not hurt. She had said, 'That is only the start of it. There will be more explosions at the second house.' Subsequently he had found a bottle or canister which had the smell of gunpowder.

The evidence of the Sergeant was followed, as all these cases were taken together in court, by that of J. J. O'Brien who, earlier in the eventful day, had been Chief Marshal at the procession. He stated that he had been walking beside the open carriage in which Asquith, his wife and daughter Violet, Redmond and the Lord Mayor were driving. A lady had come on to the back of the carriage and, when he seized her, she 'beat him in the face for all she was worth'. There was laughter in court. He went on to say that she had pulled an epaulet off his coat. There was renewed laughter. He explained that he had afterwards discovered that it was a hatchet which had been thrown and that it had struck Redmond on the ear. The accused asked him if he had not been wearing a 'sort of court dress'. No, he answered, 'I was in Robert Emmet's dress'. Again there was laughter. 'Perhaps your eye at the time deceived you ?' cross-questioned the accused, and O'Brien answered, 'You put me in a way my eyes could not deceive me.' Two of the ladies were sentenced to five years penal servitude and a third to seven months imprisonment with hard labour, but ill health, caused by prolonged hunger striking, mitigated the severity of the law.

What Asquith said in his Theatre Royal speech was, not unnaturally, overshadowed by these exciting stage effects. He discussed two objections to the Home Rule Bill — that it did not satisfy Irish nationality and that Ulster would not accept it. He was given a mixed reception. A reference in his speech to Balfour was disconcertingly received with cheers. When he asked whether Irish nationality was not quite consistent with imperial unity, some vociferous noes were mingled with the expected chorus of yes. Asked whether he would set the British army to work, and was he prepared for the certainty of civil war, he avoided the challenge and merely repeated his personal opinion that Ulster's attitude was unreasonable.

At the end of July the scene shifted again to Britain and, at the invitation of the Duke of Marlborough, to

Blenheim. The lessons of mass pageantry learnt by the Conservatives at Balmoral, near Belfast, were now to be put into practice on English soil. Special trains brought 3000 people to the quiet Oxfordshire stations nearest to Blenheim. A huge marquee was erected in which the assembled demonstrators lunched. They were shown the treasures of the Palace and then they marched in procession to the courtyard to hear Bonar Law, Carson and F. E. Smith. When the delegates were seated, the gates were thrown wide open and local people streamed in, bringing the whole gathering up to between 10,000 and 15,000.

The afternoon was warm and sunny, but there was no sunshine in the thunderous speeches. 'The concentrated essence of the fighting army of Unionism', as the Duke of Marlborough described it in opening the proceedings, proved to be as heady a dose as anything brewed across the water. Bonar Law indulged in language that, even in the excited atmosphere of the summer, startled men in all parties who held the constitutional proprieties dear. Dealing with what he dismissed as the 'intolerable' use of British troops to shoot down loyalists 'who demand no privilege which is not enjoyed by you and me, and no privilege which any one of us would ever surrender', he went on to give encouragement to the Ulster Volunteers in such terms as can never before have been used by a leader of one of the great parties in the state. And he emphasized that what he said was spoken with a full sense of the position he held as head of the Opposition. These were his words :

'While I had still in the party a position of less responsibility than that which I have now, I said that, in my opinion, if an attempt were made without the clearly expressed will of the people of this country, and as part of a corrupt parliamentary bargain, to deprive these men of their birthright, *they would be justified in resisting by all means in their power, including force.*' There were cheers as loud as if old 'Duke John' had just returned in triumph from the battlefield of Blenheim. Warmed by them, Bonar Law went on: 'I said so then, and I say now, with a full sense of the responsibility which attaches to my position, that if the attempt be made under present conditions, *I can imagine no length of resistance to which Ulster will go in which I shall not be ready to support them, and in which they will not be supported by the overwhelming majority of the British people*'. This flourishing of a blank cheque in the face of Carson, this invitation to him to fill it up in favour of civil war, brought the audience from their seats to cheer for some minutes on end.

Carson, in giving thanks for so powerful and unqualified an offer of alliance, reminded his allies of how the Irish Nationalists had rejoiced over British defeats in the Anglo-Boer war. One of them, Patrick O'Brien, to whom Asquith had just written a letter of thanks, had advised Irish troops in that war to turn round and shoot their officers. But that was not surprising, for the Irish kept Asquith in office in exchange for the surrender of his honour. Bonar Law had spoken, Carson went on, of the Prime Minister's reception in Dublin in the previous week — a reception which was refused to that Prime Minister's King. What did Asquith care about that? It was not a year since he tricked the same King. (There were cries of 'Shame'.) He would tell them why the Lord Mayor and Corporation of Dublin were afraid to mete out to the King the same welcome that they meted out to the Prime Minister. When Queen Victoria, just before her death, went over to Dublin, and the Corporation, in a fit of generosity, came forward to honour the sovereign, what did Redmond do? He made a speech in which he said the Corporation had degraded the capital of Ireland by debasing itself at the foot of a sovereign. Asquith had said he was not satisfied that Ulster was in earnest; he was satisfied that Ulster would submit. (There were cries of 'Never'.) That was a provocative challenge that Unionist Ulster would accept.

Then Carson came to the heart of his matter. 'We will shortly challenge the Government to interfere with us if they dare, and we will with equanimity await the result. We will do this regardless of all consequences of all personal loss or of all inconvenience. They may tell us if they like that that is treason. It is not for men who have such stakes as we have at issue to trouble about the cost. We are prepared to take the consequences.'

CHAPTER V

SIGNING THE COVENANT

CHURCHILL, brooding angrily over these goings on at his ancestral home, burst out in a long letter to Sir George Ritchie, the Chairman of the Liberal Party in Dundee for one of the constituencies in which he was the sitting member. He began by referring to 'the countenance and encouragement shown by the ruling Conservative leaders to doctrines of loyalist violence'. He accused Bonar Law and 'his lieutenant, Sir Edward Carson', of having, for some months past, on repeated occasions, 'incited the Orangemen to civil war upon their fellow-countrymen and, if necessary, upon the forces of the Crown; and the former has often suggested that this process in Ireland should be accompanied in England by the lynching of His Majesty's ministers. No doubt it is true that these foolish and wicked words go far beyond the intentions of the speakers, and that they would be unspeakably shocked and frightened if all this melodramatic stuff in which they are indulging were suddenly to explode into real bombs and cannon, if the ground of this peaceful kingdom were strewn with English and Irish corpses, slain in fratricidal strife, and if, instead of eagerly expecting to kiss hands on obtaining office, there was nothing before them but the bleak outlook of a felon's cell or place of execution. They would be very glad to get back from such a nightmare to their perorations under the comforting protection of the police and of the law.'

Churchill denounced the doctrines of Bonar Law as fatal to constitutional evolution and as likely to put wild

ideas into heads other than those on Irish shoulders.
'There are many millions of very poor people in this island,
divorced from the land, crowded into the back streets of
cities, forced to toil for a scanty reward through their whole
span of existence, who suffer the cruel sting and pressure
of circumstances and have little else, except their lives, to
whom these counsels of violence and mutiny may not be
unattractive and who may be lured to their own and to
public disaster by hearkening to them.   The doctrines of
Mr. Bonar Law at Blenheim are the doctrines of Mr. Ben
Tillett on Tower Hill.   But Tillett's men were starving.'

But Churchill did not end with this shrewd thrust.
'All this talk of violence,' he continued, 'of bayonets and
bullets, of rebellion and civil war, has come from one side
alone.   The Orangemen have always been notorious for
the intemperance of their language and for the religious
bigotry which explains, though it does not excuse it.   But
now we have the Conservative leader exploiting and
endorsing all their worst excesses, and committing his
party to the proposition that acts which are in themselves
cruel, wicked and contrary to law become good and praise-
worthy if they arise from a political motive.   Yet it is only
twelve years since the Conservative Government which he
supported was punishing with rigour Dutchmen who had
sided with their blood relations in the field.   And in less
than twelve months — if Home Rule were frustrated — he
might be sending Irish Nationalists to penal servitude and
the gallows, and holding three provinces of Ireland in the
grip of a Coercion Act, in the name of that same law and
order which he himself is now so reckless to trample down.'

All these exhibitions would not seduce the Government
into weakness or into violence.   'We shall pursue our path
patiently and soberly.   Our policy is benevolent, our
consciences are clear.   We are striving all we can to make
the constitution and parliamentary machinery, which is
the only substitute for anarchy or despotism, meet the needs

of the time and the cry of the people : to shield them from violence from within and from without, to give them some bulwark against sickness and unemployment, to reclaim for them some share of the land which they have lost, to guard the cheapened food which they have won.'

He closed with a recognition that, sooner or later, the Tories might come back into office. But that would not happen until their leader 'divests himself of doctrines which disqualify him and those who back him from the discharge of official responsibilities by which every lawless or disruptive movement in any part of the Empire can be justified, and from which every street bully with a brickbat and every crazy fanatic who is fumbling with a pistol may derive inspiration'.

Bonar Law, in a somewhat lame reply to this formidable onslaught, complained that Churchill had begged the question. His attack would have been applicable against his father, though Home Rule could not then have been carried without the majority of the British people. Nevertheless, the feeling of uneasiness did begin to be felt faintly in the Conservative ranks. Mr. Nicholas Cockshutt, a Lancashire Unionist candidate, protested against his leader's words, and was repudiated by the local Unionist Executive. Lord Hugh Cecil sought to put a moral gloss on the crudities of his fellow Conservatives by justifying the right of rebellion in extreme cases. Suppose, for instance, he asked, that Venice were to be handed back to Austria and, carrying his defence to casuistical lengths, he suggested that the contemplated Ulster resistance was so well organized that there would be no need for bloodshed.

By this time the high command in Ulster knew that there was no going back and that if they were to win their case they must do two things — first, show convincing proofs of their strength on the lines approved by Lord Hugh Cecil and, secondly, impose discipline on their rank-and-file. They decided to have an army backed by the whole Protestant civil population and to ensure, as far as they possibly could, that there were no stragglers or looters in it. The corner boys of Belfast must take the King's shilling as minted by King Carson. Action promptly followed, but not before there had been yet another reminder that it was nearly overdue.

On September 14 a fierce riot took place at the Celtic Park football ground. Revolvers, knives and sticks came into play. Large bodies of police were hurried to the spot, but were quite unable to keep order, and the fighting only ceased when the combatants on either side drew off. Several thousand men and boys took part and some sixty casualties were taken off to hospital. This football ground in the Nationalist quarter was the property of a Roman Catholic club — for which reason it had been the scene of Churchill's meeting in February. On this September afternoon the visiting team from Linfield, in the neighbourhood, was a Protestant one. Until half-time the greatest good-humour prevailed. But the crowd, left idle when the players retired to the pavilion at half-time, turned its thoughts to politics. Soon there were two struggling sections, one carrying a Union Jack and the other the Celtic colours. Revolver shots were heard, and the din was deafening. Telephone messages were sent for police and doctors. A couple of flags, with stripes of green and white, the Celtic colours, were carried by a crowd of yelling boys, and, on the Donegal Road side, a Union Jack was displayed. It was taken as a party challenge, and in the struggle the Celtic colours were captured. In the furious rushes hundreds were knocked down. The police charged with batons. It was thought by some optimists that, if the match could be resumed, the riot might die down. But further play was out of the question.

Shocking though all this was to peaceful folk of either colour, temptation to point its moral against the Government could not be resisted. 'Is it bluff now?' sober members of the Protestant working-class were reported to have asked, adding, 'Does the Government still think we have no firearms in Belfast?' Whatever the Government thought, Carson and Craig knew that there were enough guns about to lead to further trouble — though not nearly as many as they intended to have before they would be satisfied that their volunteers were sufficiently mobilized.

Craig, pondering in an Ulster club, had been asked by a friend what he was doing. He had answered, 'Trying to draft an oath for our people, and it is no easy matter to get at what will suit'. The friend suggested that he could not do better than take the old Scottish Covenant. The club librarian found them a copy of the Solemn League and Covenant which breathed the spirit of those Scottish forefathers of the Ulstermen who had always delighted 'to prove their doctrine orthodox by apostolic blows and knocks'. The original was too long-winded for Craig's purpose, and its religious associations made it unsuitable for use as an anti-Home Rule manifesto without the permission of the Protestant churchmen. These difficulties were overcome. A form of words, streamlined to suit 1912 taste without completely losing the strong flavour of the old Covenanters, was evolved and revised to meet clerical objections. The authorities of the Church of Ireland and of the Presbyterian, Methodist and Congregational Churches were consulted. The final text read:

Being convinced in our consciences that Home Rule would be disastrous to the material well-being of Ulster as well as the whole of Ireland, subversive of our civil and religious freedom, destructive of our citizenship, and perilous to the unity of the Empire, we, whose names are underwritten, men of Ulster, loyal subjects of His Gracious Majesty King George V, humbly relying on the God whom our fathers in days of stress and trial confidently trusted, do hereby pledge ourselves in solemn Covenant throughout this our time of threatened calamity to stand by one another in defending for ourselves and our children our cherished position of equal citizenship in the United Kingdom, and in using all means which may be found necessary to defeat the present conspiracy to set up a Home Rule Parliament in Ireland. And in the event of such a Parliament being forced upon us we further solemnly and mutually pledge ourselves to refuse to recognise its authority. In sure confidence that God will defend the right we hereto subscribe our names. And further, we individually declare that we have not already signed this Covenant. God save the King.

The Irish Unionist parliamentary party gave it their blessing and the public were somewhat informally introduced to it. Carson, bare-headed and smoking a cigarette, came out on to the steps leading to Craigavon, Craig's house, and explained what had been prepared to a large gathering of journalists. But that was the end of informality. More than 500 religious services were arranged to mark the signing of the Covenant. The hymns chosen included, 'O God, our help in ages past', 'A sure stronghold our God is He' and 'O God of Bethel'. Lessons from Isaiah, the Psalms and Ephesians were chosen, and each service concluded with the national anthem. There were processions through the Ulster towns. Carson was met outside Lisburn by men carrying lighted torches and dummy rifles. His horses were taken out of his carriage and he was escorted through the decorated and illuminated streets with pipes and drums playing 'The Boyne Water' and 'Protestant Boys' and the crowd waving Union Jacks. He was in good fettle for these celebrations. He had recently told an English audience in the more prosaic surroundings of the Criterion Restaurant that when he went over to Ireland he intended to 'break every law that is possible'.

F. E. Smith, a future Lord Chancellor, had been scarcely less emphatic in announcing that he would not shrink from the consequences of his convictions, 'not

though the whole fabric of the Commonwealth be con-
vulsed'. While Carson was touring Lisburn, the Ulster
Women's Unionist Association issued a Covenant of their
own, couched in equally forthright language. For the
benefit of their sisters in England, Scotland and Wales
who wished to sign this declaration, offices were opened in
Westminster, Manchester, York, Liverpool, Edinburgh and
Glasgow.

From place to place the peripatetic orators moved amid
mounting scenes of excitement. 'We are not to be bought
like cattle at a fair', said one speaker, arguing that Home
Rule would mean the selling of Ireland into Roman bondage.
The Liberal leaders in general and Churchill in particular
came under heavy fire. An Ulster K.C. asked his cheering
listeners, 'What do you care about the criticisms of men
who tricked their King and smashed the constitution as to
whether your action is legal or whether it is illegal?'
F. E. Smith made the same point even more plainly, saying
they might make their laws if they chose, but those laws
would not be binding upon the Unionists, and they did
not intend to obey them. This pronouncement from one
of the most eminent members of the English Bar was
greeted with cheers and cries of 'Never'.

Staff work designed to make everything ready for the
great day proceeded with gusto and efficiency. A first
consignment of seven hundred large cardboard boxes
containing the forms and other documents, sealed and
registered, was sent off on Wednesday, September 25, and
was followed up by others on the next two days. The
forms were in books of ten sheets of foolscap size, with
places on each sheet for ten signatures; on the top of
each sheet was printed the text of the Covenant. The
boxes also contained copies of the Covenant printed on
cardboard in large, bold type. These were for hanging in
the room or hall where the Covenant was to be signed.
A third version was included in each box. Printed in old

English type on parchment, and marked in crimson with the symbol of the Red Hand of Ulster, it was issued in large quantities. Every signatory was to have one to show that he had been enrolled in the Unionist force and also to keep as an heirloom to be framed and hung up in his home and bequeathed to his children. No one under sixteen might sign, and 'in the case of illiterates, or those unable to sign their own name', the name was to be written by a member of the local committee and to be initialled.

While these documents were being circulated, Carson went to Portadown. There he was met by mounted farmers wearing grey slouch hats and carrying long bamboo canes topped by Union Jack pennons in imitation of lances. Field guns made of wood, painted a steel-grey colour, were drawn through the streets and followed by a Red Cross ambulance, complete with nurses. Carson told the Portadown crowd that he had got a letter from a gentleman in Birmingham, saying that if Ulster did not now resist to the end they would prove themselves the greatest set of braggarts and blusterers in existence. When he had finished, he was presented with a blackthorn stick, decorated with orange and purple ribbons. He held this cudgel aloft, promising always to prize it, hoping that he might never have to use it, but that if he did, he would do so to the best of his ability.

On Friday, September 27, the eve of Ulster Day, messages of support streamed into the organizers from eminent persons. A pledge not to accept a seat in either House of the Irish legislature was received from a number of peers, headed by Lord Roberts, the last Commander-in-Chief of the British Army. Lord Curzon wished every success to the men and women of Ulster; Admiral the Hon. Sir E. R. Fremantle offered his sincere sympathy to Ulster in resisting by all means in her power; Admiral of the Fleet Sir Edward Seymour prophesied that Home Rule would mean financial ruin; Lord Robert Cecil

THE CAMPAIGN OPENS. CARSON'S RECEPTION AT THE ENTRANCE TO THE GROUNDS AT PORTORA HILL

described the Government as 'mere usurpers', and went on, 'If the situation results in civil war — which may Heaven avert — the responsibility will rest not on Ulster but on the government.'

The evening was marked by a meeting in the Ulster Hall outside which the watchword blazed in electric lights — Ulster will fight. Carson was twice presented — once inside the hall and once outside for the benefit of a crowd of some 25,000 people — with an historic flag. It was of faded yellow silk, and Colonel Wallace, Grand Master of the Belfast Orangemen, explained that it had been carried before William III at the Battle of the Boyne. Carson took the long staff in both hands and, shaking out the ample yellow folds, waved it to and fro. The crowd made the echoes ring with the chorus of 'Rule Britannia'.

A sceptical Catholic newspaper in Belfast remarked next day, 'If that flag ever saw the Battle of the Boyne, all we can say is that the man who manufactured it deserves undying fame for the strength and durability of the material'. But this heresy was drowned by the indignant protests of true believers, who asserted that the flag had been carried at the battle by a Lieutenant Watson, in the possession of whose descendants it had, until quite recently, remained. There was a red star in its centre and at one of the top corners the cross of St. George. Concession to disbelief was made that it was probably the personal emblem of the family and not the flag of an army in the old wars. Whatever its origins may have been, it was now on active service.

Proceedings on Covenant Day began with prayers, hymns, lessons and a sermon preached by an ex-Moderator of the General Assembly of the Irish Presbyterian Church. Behind his pulpit was a guard of honour and the flag that had (or had not) crossed Boyne Water. After this religious prelude, Carson and his principal lieutenants signed the Covenant under fire from photographers. A silver pen was used, which Carson handed to London-derry whose signature was followed in order by those of the Moderator of the General Assembly, the Bishop of Down (afterwards Primate of All Ireland), the Dean of Belfast, afterwards Bishop of Down, the General Secretary of the Presbyterian Church, the President of the Methodist Conference, and the ex-Chairman of the Congregational Union. Then the doors were opened to the general public, who came in in batches of four or five hundred at a time, to sign their names. A few of the signatures were in blood. One of the donors claimed that he followed a family tradition, as he was the lineal descendant of an ancestor who had signed the Solemn League and Covenant in that bloody way in Stuart times.

At the close of a stirring day Carson left for Liverpool. As he crossed the gangway at Belfast under an immense Union Jack, a parting salute of revolver shots had been fired in his honour. As his ship, the *Patriotic*, headed for the open sea, bonfires blazed on both arms of Belfast Lough and ships anchored in the channel sent up rockets in showers of red, white and blue sparks. Alderman Salvidge was waiting on the landing-stage at Liverpool with an address of welcome on behalf of the Working Men's Conservative Association. Carson shook him by the hand, saying: 'I bring a message from the democracy of Belfast to the democracy of Liverpool'. The Lancashire crowd sang 'O God, our help in ages past'.

Other cities in England and Scotland had joined in the signing of the Covenant. In Edinburgh the ceremony took place on the 'Covenanters' Stone' in the old Grey-friars churchyard. From Liverpool, Carson went in triumph to Glasgow where a loyal supporter described him as having 'moved hundreds to tears'. The excitement spread to Rottingdean, which was illuminated for Carson's home-coming. He told his neighbours that some base

L.E.A.

SIR EDWARD CARSON SIGNS THE COVENANT ON ULSTER DAY

L.E.A.

THE LADIES SIGN

fellows had said that he ought to be prosecuted. 'They know where I am,' he continued, 'I am always ready! The only reason they give why I am not prosecuted is that if I am there might be riots — the most extraordinary reason for not carrying out the law that I ever heard.'

F

CHAPTER VI

THE HOME RULE BILL

GAINST this melodramatic background Parliament reassembled, and the Government settled down to force the Bill through by uninhibited use of the guillotine. Their scheme was technically involved and fiercely contested. It was a mixture of 'compartment' and 'kangaroo' closure. Twenty-five days were allowed for the Committee, five for the Report and two for the Third Reading. Discussion in committee had to close on some days at 7.30 or at 10.30 P.M., on any day the Chairman might select and pass over amendments. Dilatory motions were to be admissible only from the Government and would be put without debate. Asquith said how much he disliked having to rush matters in this fashion, but the Government meant to get the Bill through in a reasonable time and to afford adequate opportunity for debate on its essential features; the Opposition meant to smother it with amendments. He thought he was being, if anything, too generous. Bonar Law gloomily replied that here were the first-fruits of the Parliament Act. The Government was determined to pass the Bill without submitting it to the electors. Tempers on either side of the House were not improved by the inopportune appearance at this point of time of the scandal (as its critics thought it to be) of the Marconi affair.

On November 11 a further cause of friction arose. The Government was defeated by 228 votes to 206 on an amendment to the financial resolution on which the Home Rule Bill was based. This happened on a snap division without any warning to the rank-and-file, though cleverly planned tactics were behind it. As soon as Mr. Mitchell-Thomson hurried in with the numbers he had checked in the lobby, some of the younger Conservatives began to shout excitedly, 'We've won'. Amendment papers and hats were thrown high into the air, and cheer upon cheer went up from the Opposition benches. There followed a few moments of hushed and tense silence until the Clerk at the table handed the slip of paper with the official figures of the division to Sir Frederick Banbury to announce. As the official slip is always handed to the victorious tellers, before Sir Frederick could say a word, pandemonium was loose.

Those on the sparsely attended Front Bench heard cries of 'Resign, resign'. A moment later, Asquith walked in from the other side of the Speaker's chair. Among the audible cries with which he was greeted were: 'Take your pension', 'Bang goes your four hundred a year', 'Go to the country and see what the country will say to you', 'Good-bye, good-bye'. The storm did not die down that day.

Asquith declared that his defeat did not represent the considered judgment of the House, and he reminded the wrathful Bonar Law that Balfour had stayed in office in somewhat similar circumstances in 1905. But this did not pacify the Conservatives. 'Many members', one observer noted, 'were obviously hysterical.' Asquith was called a traitor, and the Speaker intervened to say that he wished that he knew who was the hon. member who had used that expression. Sir William Bull rose with 'I used the word'. Craig supported him with 'I echo everything said by the honourable member', and again Sir William Bull shouted 'Traitor'. The Speaker told him that if he persisted in disregarding the authority of the chair, he must be asked to leave the House. Bull stuck to his point and walked out.

As the broil developed, the Speaker vainly interposed

by reminding members who were calling out, 'Adjourn, adjourn', that they had appealed over and over again for fair play. 'They have not given it us,' retorted Austen Chamberlain. 'Civil war, civil war,' cried George Wyndham. The rhythmic beat of 'Adjourn, Adjourn' was drowned in the shouts that arose from all parts of the House and that made it impossible for the Attorney-General to make himself heard. Finally the Speaker interposed again, saying in serious tones, 'In my opinion, grave disorder has arisen'. An Irish member interjected with 'I should say so!' The House was adjourned under Standing Order 21. After an hour, the Speaker returned to the chair, but still the Attorney-General was howled down. And so was the Speaker. 'No Home Rule', 'No more business at Westminster'.

Ten minutes of this was enough for the Speaker, who again adjourned the House, this time until the next day. The Opposition greeted this with triumphant cheers and more waving of hats, handkerchiefs and papers. As Churchill and Seely were going out together, they were taunted with the chorus of 'Rats, rats'. Churchill waved a handkerchief to encourage the Liberals to cheer the Prime Minister, and, before he put it back in his pocket, he waved it towards the Opposition. Ronald McNeill, an Ulster member, seized from the side of the chair a small bound copy of the Orders and threw it at Churchill, striking him on the forehead. Churchill started angrily, but was restrained by two members. He left the chamber, in which tension was relieved by Will Crooks jovially asking, 'Should auld acquaintance be forgot?' They slept on it, and then, feeling a little ashamed of the exhibition he had made of himself, McNeill made a handsome apology which was handsomely accepted by Churchill, thus rounding off the incident in a traditional manner that, in those days, was being more honoured in the breach than in the observance. The Speaker, Lowther (later Lord

Ullswater), kept the missile as a souvenir, remarking that 'a bent corner of the leather binding bears evidence of the improper use to which it had been applied'.

This was in mid-November, and was followed by a series of relatively dull debates. But there was another milder ripple of excitement over the proposed use of the Union Jack as the official flag to fly over the Irish Parliament House daily during its sessions. Mr. MacVeagh, the Nationalist member for County Down, objecting to this, aroused some indignation by his version of the historical origins of the flag and by stating that Unionist members got information about Ireland from a Mr. Rosenbaum, who was employed by their party organizers and attended under the gallery during debates. He was reproved by Balfour for trying to make the Union Jack ridiculous, and Redmond poured oil on the troubled waters by saying that under Home Rule the Union Jack and the Irish flag would fly together.

The year closed with the House reassembling on December 30, still in the throes of the Report stage. Tempers, frayed and wearied by this long-drawn-out controversy of which the end was far from being in sight, were worsened at the beginning of January by yet another cause of friction. Lloyd George fell foul of the doctors over his health scheme, and was violently denounced by 1200 of them assembled at the Queen's Hall. There he was called 'a moral leper' and the doctors who had agreed to go on to his new panel were sneered at as 'blacklegs'. This was regarded as yet another proof that the Liberal Government had determined to undermine the foundations on which the social structure of Britain had always rested. The House had thus been ruffled by the prospect of a lowering of the status of the medical profession when it had to turn its attention yet again to Home Rule.

Carson now held out a branch with some meagre olives on it. He moved an amendment excluding 'the province of Ulster' from the Bill, but, as he went on to give an assurance that it would be opposed as much as ever, and to attack its 'putrid finance', he did nothing to lower the temperature. Bonar Law, who supported him, said that the amendment would get rid of the resistance of Ulster. But he too was still truculent. Ulster, he said, would prefer foreign to Nationalist rule. Ulstermen were quite willing to risk their lives, and if they were shot by British soldiers, the Government would fall. Churchill hit back at him, laughing at the 'latest Tory threat — Ulster will secede to Germany'.

As the debates continued, attendance in the House dwindled, and it was a relief when the Bill was passed on to its certain doom in the Lords. All that had happened to it in Committee as the result of these interminable discussions was that the supremacy of the Imperial Parliament over future Irish affairs had been strengthened and emphasized. Balfour, giving it a parting kick towards another place, prophesied that if Yorkshiremen were put in the position of Ulstermen, they would spend their days in drilling and their nights in importing arms, and he drew an analogy between Ulster in 1913 and the American colonies in Washington's time.

Balfour's suavity did not prevent him from having a sense of occasion and he was not going to allow all the rude things to be said by his Tory colleagues. He too was rude, but he had a way of stylizing rudeness. Lord Riddell, always quick to gather good stories, as became the proprietor of the *News of the World*, noted in his diary what Bonar Law had said to him about this Balfourian speech. When Balfour sat down — so the Conservative leader told the newspaper proprietor — Austen Chamberlain leant over to someone on the Front Bench and said, 'That is the advantage of having a reputation for good manners. Bonar Law could not have said that!' 'I doubt if Bonar Law is very fond of Balfour', Riddell cynically confided to the pages of his diary. 'I gather this from small indications. He said someone had remarked that, when Balfour retired, he would be placed on a pedestal, but that someone else had added that the disadvantage of being on a pedestal was that you were liable to fall off.'

So, after fifty-two days in the Commons, the Bill was allowed briefly to run the gauntlet of their Lordships. They put down a barrage on it from all angles. Lord St. Aldwyn, opening the debate, complained that Irish administration cost £1,500,000 more than Irish revenue yielded because the ministers had brought in Old Age Pensions and Insurance Acts applicable to Ireland although they knew that they were soon going to bring in Home Rule. The Archbishop of York eloquently lamented the 'grim, determined, menacing' attitude of Ulster and pleaded with ministers to go to the country and to find out what the electorate thought. Their Lordships threw the Bill out by 326 to 69.

This was at the end of January, and simultaneously the special Commission set up in Ulster to prepare a scheme for a provisional Government presented its draft report. It allowed for a 'central authority' under which the whole business of government would be carried on in defiance of the Home Rule Bill if it ever became law. There was no lack of eminent men to serve in this government. The Archbishop of Armagh, the Moderator of the General Assembly of the Presbyterian Church in Ireland, legal luminaries and high-ranking naval and military officers agreed to give their services. An ironical touch was added to these preparations for resistance to an Act of Parliament by the draft ordinance which was to bring them into force, beginning, 'It is Hereby Enacted by the Central Authority in the name of the King's Most Excellent Majesty that . . .'

A minor set-back occurred to the Orange cause through the loss of a by-election at Londonderry to the Home Rulers, who got in by 57 votes in a poll of more than 95

per cent of the electorate. Protestant Ulster stiffened
itself by listening to stories that every available elector had
polled, even the dying, and that priests had attended some
Nationalist voters to give them, if necessary, Extreme
Unction. A parliamentary lull followed the rejection of the
Bill by the Lords, until it turned up again at midsummer
in the Commons.

Five days before it did so, on June 9, an important
step forward had been taken in the resistance movement.
Lord Roberts ('Bobs' to the public that idealized the little
V.C. Field-Marshal) wrote as odd a letter as ever can
have been penned by a senior officer holding the King's
commission. He wrote from Ascot to another old soldier,
Colonel Hickman, a member of Parliament, in the following terms:

DEAR HICKMAN,

I have been a long time finding a Senior Officer to help
in the Ulster business, but I think I have got one now. His
name is Lieut.-General Sir George Richardson, K.C.B., c/o
Messrs. Henry S. King & Co., Pall Mall, S.W. He is a retired
Indian officer, active and in good health. He is not an Irishman, but has settled in Ireland. . . . Richardson will be in
London for about a month, and is ready to meet you at any
time.

I am sorry to read about the capture of rifles.

Believe me,

Yours sincerely,

ROBERTS

Two seizures of arms had just taken place. The one at
Dublin had been sent from Liverpool to Lord Farnham
and the other, at Belfast, consisting of twelve cases of over
a thousand rifles with bayonets attached, had been shipped
from Manchester to Liverpool as 'electrical plant' and
consigned 'to order'. The cases had not been officially
seized in the first place, but were detained owing to
misdescription and misdirection to await the arrival of the
consignee to claim them. Nervous citizens in northern

Ireland began, at this point, to make enquiries about
insurance against riot risks. One resident in Belfast
found that insurance offices were willing to cover his
private house against the possibility of direct damage
caused by riots or civil commotion. Actuarial opinion was
divided. Some offices would cover fire risk for a premium
of five shillings per cent, but were not disposed to commit
themselves for a longer period than twelve months. Other
offices would cover all such risks for a premium of five
shillings per cent and would accept the risk for two years
at ten shillings per cent provided that the property was
not owned by a political leader or was not, for any other
reason, specially liable to attack. Underwriters were submitted to a brisk fire of enquiries.

Richardson was a man after the Ulstermen's own hearts.
He had been with Roberts in Afghanistan in the late
'seventies, had commanded a flying column in the Tirah
expedition in the 'nineties and a cavalry brigade against
the Boxers in China. For the past six years — since he
had relinquished the command of a division at Poona — he
had been in retirement. Now he found himself in Belfast
at the head of a force of between fifty and sixty thousand
men with recruiting in brisk progress. This influential
military support from across the channel justified Carson
in telling the Government, as a little later he publicly did,
'that we have pledges and promises from some of the
greatest generals in the army who have given their word
that, when the time comes, if it is necessary, they will come
over and help us to keep the old flag flying'.

At the same time as Richardson appeared, some
further spiritual support was forthcoming. The Presbyterian Assembly of Ireland debated, by 921 to 43, a
resolution declaring that the opposition of the Church to
Home Rule was as determined and unyielding as in 1886
and in 1893. 131,000 Presbyterians signed a memorial
against the Bill.

Back it came for another second reading in the Commons. Asquith deplored the 'blank, summary, uncompromising negative' of the Lords. But he said nothing about any concessions to Ulster. Balfour, taking on the role of Cassandra, drew a parallel between the impending collision and the loss of the *Victoria* and *Camperdown*. 'Let members search their consciences,' he said, 'and see if in the cause of the Bill they mean to shoot down Ulstermen.' Carson was in jaunty form. The Irish Unionists would refuse to help to play out the pantomime. 'You may jeer at us, but we will go on, and eventually will defeat you. . . . You are crying peace where there is no peace. You know it, and you will fail.' Again the faithful Bonar Law followed him, asking again why not have an election ? The Nationalist attitude was that of Moslems — 'Be my brother or I will slay thee'.

By July the Lords had their return match, hitting out, as before, all round the wicket. Curzon declared that a flame would be kindled that would rush through the country like a forest fire and would not stop until (boldly confusing his metaphor) ministers were extinguished. After Morley had sought to persuade the hostile majority facing him on the scarlet benches that a General Election before the Bill passed would be a far greater interference with parliamentary authority than anything in the Parliament Act, the Lords played their last card. They rejected the Bill.

It was their final chance under the constitution as it had been revised so distastefully from the Conservative point of view. The Bill would become law unless the King refused to give it his consent. Would he ? That was a question that had been exercising the minds of Conservative leaders — and of the King himself. He was now to take an increasingly active part in negotiations and to be looked to from all sides. All sides were beginning to realize that matters had gone too far and that, unless terms

could be reached which would save the faces of all concerned, there was no knowing where this speechifying and
military manœuvring would end. How the King came to
do his sensible best in the summer and autumn of 1913 to
restore sanity to British politics will be discussed in the
next chapter. Before describing the manner in which he
handled his ministers and their opponents, as a shrewd
family doctor deals with a neurotic but otherwise healthy
patient, some other developments must be recorded.

True to form, the Ulstermen had given a stirring
preview to the obsequies of the Bill in the House of Lords.
They had marked the week-end before its final, mournful
passage through the Upper House by celebrating July 12
with an even bigger and better procession. The Grand
Orange Lodge of Belfast had organized it, and it had taken
nearly two and a half hours to pass. Carson and Wallace
were at its head in a carriage, and there had been the now
familiar fiery speeches. But that was not all. While
Carson urged the people of Ulster not to pay taxes to
support a government of the Ancient Order of Hibernians,
there were what even the newspapers in sympathy with the
Orange cause admitted to have been 'regrettable incidents'.
Stones and bottles were thrown. At least one skull was
fractured. Nervousness about where such rough-houses
were heading led to a stiffening in public in both camps.
Supporters of the Government asked angrily why Carson
and his followers who were so openly defying law and order
were not arrested. Even the gentle Spender held that the
limit had been passed, and that what was sauce for Tom
Mann and the Labour geese should be sauce for the
Ulster ganders.

But the Government were not such fools as to attempt
to bring Carson to trial. Spender protested that 'Englishmen looked on amazed at the spectacle of Sir Edward
Carson, a pillar of British law, solemnly accepting office
as head of a provisional government which was preparing

to levy war on Parliament, and reviewing his forces with another distinguished lawyer, Mr. F. E. Smith, acting as aide-de-camp and galloper'.

It was one of the rare occasions on which Spender and the Prime Minister did not see eye to eye. Asquith, in a reply to this criticism, delivered, as Spender subsequently reflected, 'with some severity', remained — and for very good reasons — adamant. Asquith protested that his decision to abstain from putting the criminal law in motion against Carson and his associates did not arise 'from timidity, nor from dilatoriness'. He, no less than Carson, was a wise lawyer, and he reflected that the machinery of a state prosecution should never be set in motion 'if its failure to score a conviction is a foregone conclusion'. He agreed that it would have been easy to draw up an indictment in respect of what had been said and done in Ireland. The charges could have been framed so as to be technically watertight, 'and they could have been proved up to the hilt by clear and indeed uncontroverted evidence'. The callowest junior at the bar would have had no difficulty up to this stage. But, as Asquith, with undeniably good sense behind him, continued, 'the guilt or innocence of the accused would be ultimately determined by a jury, and, as the days of jury-packing were happily over, it was as certain as any of the sequences of nature that no Irish jury would convict'. Asquith, with tantalizing and characteristic reticence, refrained from speculating on what would have happened had an English jury been asked to give its opinion on, say, the speeches made, thanks to the hospitality of the Duke of Marlborough, at Blenheim.

Asquith's doubts were matched by Tory misgivings. Faced with that July skull-cracking, *The Times* expressed its fears in a frank leading article. 'The Ulster Covenant', it wrote, 'was signed by soldiers as it was signed by most distinguished judges and they entertain the reasonable fear that even before the Home Rule Bill can pass into law, the Government may be compelled to bring the troops into collision with the forces of the Unionists in Ireland. Should the Bill be passed next May, the army will then be confronted by a situation more serious still; and it is notorious that some officers have already begun to speak of sending in their papers.'

Reading between the lines of these diverse judgments, it may be seen that a measure of common ground was being reached. All concerned were beginning to search for an excuse for compromise. The pantomime, as Carson had called it, had been played too long, and there was an increasingly uneasy suspicion that before the curtain went down on it, it might turn into tragedy. For this reason, interest shifted in the late summer and autumn from Parliament and the public places of Ulster to Balmoral (the Scottish and not the Ulster one), and, unknown at first to the world, to Mr. Max Aitken's house in Surrey.

CHAPTER VII

ENTER THE KING

THE King's post at Buckingham Palace was swelled in these months by a spate of letters, many of them impassioned and anonymous, appealing to him to intervene on behalf of his loyal Protestant citizens. His biographer, Sir Harold Nicolson, has written that the cry went up, 'Surely the King is not going to hand us over to the Pope'. In vain Lord Stamfordham had sought to set his mind at rest with 'Pray, Sir, do not give a thought to the irresponsible and, as a rule, anonymous letter writers who dare to address their cowardly and insulting words to you'.

The King's mind was not set at rest. He had been following events closely with a cool, common-sense eye. He was kept well informed of what was happening by people in all, or almost all, camps. Elder statesmen, with one important exception, rained advice upon him. The exception was Asquith, who refrained, until the King required him to do so, from bringing the Crown into the controversy.

But before the end of July the King had seen the Irish Secretary, Birrell, who had proved to be more than usually wrapped in the mists. Birrell had declared the situation to be artificial, had discounted the seriousness of the state of things in Ulster, and had accused Carson — not an Orangeman, a Dublin man — of having lost his head. 'As to fighting, there would be no one to fight.' Birrell told the King that he would be ready to accept a proposal from the Opposition for Ulster to contract out of the Bill.

'Mr. Redmond would never agree to this plan,' said the King. 'He would have to agree,' said Birrell. 'But he would turn you out'; to which Birrell retorted, 'Let him — damn good thing if he did.' The King drew little comfort from this ministerial advice, and not much more from the collective and conflicting wisdom of his Conservative advisers.

They brought a heavy weight of pressure on the King in an effort to persuade him that it was his constitutional duty, now that the power of the House of Lords had been so unfairly destroyed, to compel an election. Lansdowne was emphatic in support of the theory that the King would be within his rights if he forced a dissolution or insisted on a referendum. Bonar Law held a similar view. He argued that the King ought to give his people a chance to say what they thought about it all before Home Rule became the law of the land. Balfour put up a more dialectical case. He distinguished between a situation in which the King was opposed to his ministers and one in which he held that the country should be consulted, although he himself was neutral or, perhaps, in agreement with ministers. He would be wrong to insist on an election in the first instance, and right to do so in the second. As Balfour regarded the Home Rule issue as being an example of his second category, he came down in favour of the King writing an open letter to the people, telling them why he had plumped for an election, and assuring them that he was ready to accept their verdict. If that course were followed, Balfour was satisfied that the prestige of the Crown would not suffer.

Other eminent men shrank back from advising so positive an exercise of the Prerogative. Rosebery described refusal to give the royal assent to the Bill as being unconstitutional and amounting to a *coup d'état*. He would go no further than recommending the King to press for an all-party conference. Loreburn and Cromer were

against the King acting against the advice of his ministers.
They thought he should tell them in writing that he bowed
to them against his better judgment and that he feared
that they were heading for civil war. Esher, who was a
tireless writer and always happy to give advice on public
matters, spread himself in a long memorandum on the
use of the Prerogative which won him an hour and a half
alone with the King. He repeated to the King what
Morley and Harcourt had told him about the probable
consequences of the Government being dismissed. They
had prophesied that in the ensuing election Home Rule
would not be mentioned. The only question would be,
'Is the country governed by the King or by the people?'
Every minister from Asquith downwards, and including
Grey, would attack the King personally. Esher was
certain that this was a correct judgment. The only
minister whom he was inclined to acquit of being likely
to attack the King was Crewe.

On August 11 Asquith was summoned to the royal
presence. The King had given much preliminary thought
as to what he should say to the Prime Minister and,
clearing his own mind, had come to the conclusion that
there ought to be a General Election before Home Rule,
but that Asquith would prefer to resign rather than to agree
to a dissolution. These reflections did not spring from
any resentment against Asquith, whom the King liked as
he did not like Bonar Law. When Asquith arrived, he
was handed a memorandum in the royal handwriting.
The most poignant paragraphs in this terse and wise
document were brief. They read, 'Whatever I do, I shall
offend half the population' and 'I cannot help feeling
that the Government is drifting and taking me with it'.
Would it not be possible to secure 'a settlement by
consent?' the King asked.

Asquith took what the King had written away with him
and, having brooded over it, sent his considered reply in

two parts. First he disposed in thorough constitutional lawyer's fashion of the theory that the veto of the Crown might now be exercised. It had not been exercised for two centuries. If it were now, whatever the pedants might say, the Crown would become 'the football of contending factions', and that, Asquith incontrovertibly added, 'is a constitutional catastrophe which it is the duty of every wise statesman to do the utmost in his power to avert'. Secondly, he minimized the chances of trouble in Ulster. There was serious danger of 'organized disorder' but not of its attaining the dimensions of civil war. A General Election before the Bill became law would make nonsense of the Parliament Act. He did not come out flat against a conference, but observed gloomily that 'an unbridgeable chasm of principle' yawned between the two sides, and he was not hopeful of finding any basis for a conference.

This was not good enough for the King, who replied in a private letter from Balmoral on September 22. By that time the King had had a series of intimate talks with guests he had invited to Scotland. They included Bonar Law, Crewe, Grey, Lansdowne, Churchill, Balfour and Harcourt. While they were at Balmoral they naturally talked things over among themselves, and in a mood very different from that of the platforms. Asquith had learnt of a morning game of golf at which Bonar Law had proposed a conversation 'confidential, personal and informal' with Liberal fellow guests, and had agreed that the tenor of what was said at it should be passed on to the Prime Minister. Asquith was told that Bonar Law had unburdened himself to this effect: 'At some time in the near future Carson will announce that, on the passage of the Home Rule Bill, he will set up a Provisional Government, call out his volunteers and take definite action to usurp the functions of the police and the guards and thus create a situation which will compel, as he believes, the armed intervention of the troops. Parliamentary opposition will,

G

if the worst comes to the worst, go to all lengths. . . .
In the circumstances, they believe, and say they have
reason to believe, that the army will not obey the Government and that a situation will be created in which a
dissolution will be forced. Bonar Law recoils from these
desperate measures. . . . I must admit that the remarkable conversation of which I have given you some account
has altered my views about a conference considerably. . . .
I have always wished to see Ulster provided for, and you
will remember how Lloyd George and I pressed its
exclusion upon the Cabinet (and how Loreburn repulsed
us in the most bloodthirsty manner).'

With this strong evidence before him that Bonar Law
was growing uneasy about the lengths to which his fiery
Irish lieutenant was prepared to go, Asquith considered
the King's letter. He was asked in it some straight
questions. 'Do you propose to employ the army to
suppress such disorders? . . . Will it be wise, will it be
fair to the Sovereign, as head of the Army, to subject the
discipline and, indeed, the loyalty of his troops to such a
strain?' If he was prepared to answer these questions in
the affirmative, then, 'you will, I am sure, bear in mind
that ours is a voluntary Army; our Soldiers are none the
less Citizens; by birth, religion and environment they may
have strong feelings on the Irish question; outside
influence may be brought to bear upon them; they see
distinguished retired Officers already organizing local
forces in Ulster; they hear rumours of Officers on the
Active List throwing up their Commissions to join this
force'. Sticking to the point that seemed to him most
material, the King closed with, 'I rejoice to know that you
are ready and anxious to enter into a conference if a
definite basis could be found upon which to confer'.

Two days after the date of the King's letter, the Ulster
Unionist Council assembled in Belfast to put the final
touches to the setting up of their Provisional Government.

They announced, after their meeting, which was in private, that they would make public their detailed plans regarding all matters necessary for repudiating and resisting the decrees of the Nationalist Parliament or Executive, and for taking over the government of Ulster in trust for the British nation at latest on the date on which the Home Rule Bill was placed upon the Statute Book.

At the same time a fund was launched to provide for the indemnifying of members of the Ulster Volunteer Force; it was to amount to at least £1,000,000. Next day the quarter-million mark had already been reached, with Carson and Londonderry, each having subscribed £10,000, bracketed at the head of the list. A Mr. George Moore, a prominent Belfast Unionist, writing to Carson to put him down for a modest £5000, lamented that 'I am but a poor man', going on, 'but how I long today for one reason, and for one reason only, to be a millionaire, namely to set an example to our real millionaires to break any etiquette that prohibits one from outdoing your own magnificent figure of £10,000'. Sir Samuel McCaughey telegraphed from Australia inviting the Treasurer of the Indemnity Fund to call upon him 'for any sum necessary'. Sir Samuel was reputed to be one of Australia's best-known millionaires, having acquired, since he emigrated from County Antrim, vast flocks of sheep. This self-made man was hailed as being typical in sentiment of Ulstermen scattered up and down the Empire.

Special religious services to mark the formal organization of the Provisional Government were held. Whatever surprises were being kept back until the worst came to the worst — and the Bill was passed — it was plain that this government was a thorough one. It now consisted of a military council and of four committees to deal respectively with the Volunteers, local subjects, education and customs, excise and postal services. On each committee there was to be a member of the Ulster Women's Unionist Council.

Sceptics noted that while Carson was supported in his membership of the Central Authority by a marquis, a duke and several peers, there was not one working man among them.

The Secretary of the Board of Trade laughed it off, saying that 'King Carson' would get no revenue, that the British and United States Post Offices would not deal with that of Ulster, that the whole scheme would break down at once and that the only reason why the Government did not prosecute was because it did not want King Carson to become St. Carson. He assured his audience, boldly but vaguely, that the Government would know how to deal with the situation.

Redmond, speaking in the deep south of County Kerry, declared that he could not go into a conference in which the principle of Home Rule would be put into the melting-pot. What Redmond said did not unduly perturb Asquith as he considered the new turn of events. The Irish leader could, and certainly would, create difficulties about re-vising the Bill to meet northern objections. Still, in the last analysis, the Government held the whip hand over its disunited Nationalist supporters in Parliament. If they were obstinate, they would have to be reminded of the only alternative open to them — either they supported the Liberals and accepted, however reluctantly, some truncated version of Home Rule, or else they must be prepared to bring the ministry down and face another spell of con-servatism in office. And that might mean no Home Rule at all.

Asquith, in weighing up the reasons in favour of making an approach to Bonar Law, found another one in southern Ireland that was more compelling than anything Redmond and his followers said. Violence had broken out in the south in August. It took the form of ugly labour troubles fermented by James Larkin, a Liverpool man who had come into prominence a few years previously by organizing the dock workers in Belfast. He was now a leading spirit in the Irish Transport Workers' Union, and he had brought together a remarkable miscellany drawn from various classes of ill-paid labour. Larkin was a successful organizer, a spellbinding orator and extremely popular with the Irish masses. He was believed to be descended from the Larkin who was one of the Fenians known as the Manchester Martyrs, executed in the 'sixties for the murder of a policeman.

Larkin's activities had brought him into conflict with the Dublin Tramway Company, whose chairman threatened a lock-out unless the men withdrew from the union. Larkin's oratorical reaction was violent, and, in the early hours of August 28, he and four other Dublin labour leaders were arrested in their beds and brought up before a magistrate on the charges of seditious libel and seditious conspiracy. The prosecuting barrister said that the Crown stood aloof from all questions of trade disputes and agitations, but could not allow speeches that were 'criminally and flagrantly illegal'. Larkin had told the crowd he was addressing that the chairman of the tramways was 'an infamous scoundrel'. He had said that the authorities were bringing in the Buffs, but that, if that was so, he was ready to 'wipe the whole of them off the streets'. Later he had said that Carson had advised the people of Ulster to arm and that he did not see any reason why the workers whom he addressed should not also arm.

The defendants were sent forward for trial, but released on bail after giving an undertaking not, meanwhile, to hold any illegal meetings or to use inflammatory language. Street fighting on a large scale promptly followed. Some hundreds of people, including a number of police officers, were injured. Stones and broken bottles were showered on the police. A company of the Royal West Kent regiment turned out and drove off the rioters.

Larkin had announced his intention of holding a

meeting of the tramway strikers in Sackville Street (now-adays called O'Connell Street) 'in spite of the police and military'. Having publicly burned a copy of the pro-clamation prohibiting the holding of this meeting, he vowed to turn up in Sackville Street 'dead or alive'. Precautions were taken to prevent him doing so in either state. But he succeeded. On the night of Saturday, August 30, he telephoned to a hotel and reserved two rooms for himself in the name of 'Donnelly and niece'. On the Sunday afternoon a taxi-cab drove up containing apparently a feeble old gentleman and a lady. The former (who, it subsequently transpired, had been wearing a false beard) was helped upstairs to the smoking-room, from which he stepped out on to the balcony. With a wave of his arm, Larkin — for it was he — attracted the attention of the crowd and, after speaking a few words, went back into the hotel, where he was arrested.

Larkin's escapade came as an ugly reminder that more had to be reckoned with in southern Ireland than the docile members of the Nationalist Party. At this stage the trouble was industrial, but no trouble in Ireland could be kept clear in the long run of nationalism. Redmond, no less than Asquith, was disturbed by this development. It was worsened, in English eyes, by the attitude towards it of the Trades Union Congress. That body showed itself prepared to be as sympathetic towards Larkin and his strikers as the Conservatives were to Carson and his Volunteers. Keir Hardie went to Dublin in the Labour cause, and his visit was denounced as being an impertinence.

The last had by no means been heard of Larkin, but order was temporarily restored and Asquith was proceeding with his reassessment of the whole situation. He was given, within a few days of the troubles in Dublin, yet further stimulus towards an inter-party settlement. Lore-burn emerged from his retirement to make an appeal to the nation that was heard on all sides with respect. It was

a lengthy appeal, taking up more than three columns of
The Times. Loreburn began by pointing out that it was
no use 'lecturing one another or explaining the enormity
of each other's conduct or policy'. It was an extravagance
to speak of civil war, or to fancy that troops, if called upon,
would refuse to maintain order; but if the Bill were passed,
there would be serious rioting, and there was a general
belief that the Conservative party in England was prepared
to condone, if not to approve it. 'A prospect of impunity',
the letter tartly continued, 'naturally encourages the
fermentation of disorder.'

The gist of Loreburn's argument was that the Bill must
be prevented from getting on to the Statute Book next
June, and that the only way to do this was to have a
conference or direct communication between the leaders.
Such a solution was in the interests of the people of Great
Britain, who 'are entitled to some say in this business'.
There was a somewhat lofty air of being above the battle
about this letter which intensely annoyed Churchill and
Lloyd George, who well remembered how its author, while
he had still been Lord Chancellor, had vigorously opposed
their policy of excluding Ulster from the start.

As soon as Asquith had read the letter, he wrote to
Loreburn asking him to tell him precisely what he meant.
He expressed himself in sympathy with the spirit of the
appeal, but feared that Carson and Redmond were not
likely to accept an invitation to come into a room and sit
round a table 'for the purpose of talking in the air about
the government of Ireland or about Federalism and
devolution'. It was no good blinding one's eyes to obvious
and undeniable facts, one of which was that four-fifths
of Ireland, with the support of a substantial British
majority in the present and late House of Commons, would
be content with nothing less than a subordinate legislature
with a local executive responsible to it. If that were agreed
upon by all concerned — and Asquith doubted whether

anything so desirable was likely to happen — he would be prepared to compromise. There was no point — finance, Ulster, Second Chamber representation and minorities — on which he was not ready and anxious to yield to any responsible suggestion.

In this mood, and at the beginning of October, he went to Balmoral where he remained for three days, sticking to his point that Carson's behaviour ruled out a conference between party leaders. Such a meeting would, he thought, be either 'a tea party or a bear-garden'. He was asked by the King an awkward question: was not the threat to coerce Ulster 'un-English and contrary to all Liberal and democratic principles?' The upshot of his visit was that the Prime Minister wrote, with the King's blessing, confidentially inviting Bonar Law to meet him. It was obvious that such a meeting must, in the inflamed state of party warfare, be private. Anything that could have been made to look like a public *anschluss* between the Government and the Opposition would have enraged hot-heads and embarrassed both leaders.

Fortunately Bonar Law had in Max Aitken a fellow Canadian and ardent admirer who was, at that date, scarcely known to the country at large. He had already begun to climb up the ladder which, with the help of the *Daily Express* and his natural gifts of wit and charm, was to bring him, as Lord Beaverbrook, into the Upper House. But that time was not yet, and Asquith and Bonar Law were able to meet conveniently and unnoticed on the neutral ground of his Surrey home. He has reported that it was not an easy meeting. When the two statesmen met on October 14 in a room overlooking the hills and the Weald around Leatherhead, there was ice in the atmosphere. Asquith sought to break it by making some preliminary comments on the beauty of the view, but, as the host has remarked, 'Bonar Law was not a scenery man'. Aitken tactfully intervened with a story, doing something a little to raise the temperature, which still remained frigid.

Asquith always took a patronizing line towards Bonar Law, whom he regarded as 'kindly and peaceable' by nature and 'a reluctant but conscientious fire-eater in public'. Bonar Law's kindliness was real and not inconsistent with toughness in negotiation. Asquith got no change out of him under Max Aitken's roof, and he got no change out of Asquith. They met twice more, on November 6 and on December 10, and at the end of it all the gap between them was as wide as ever. They were able to exchange sympathy on their respective diehards. Asquith was candid about the Irish Party and the headaches it gave him. Bonar Law said that he was not sure that his were not even greater; he had to reckon not only with Carsonism (as distinguished from Carson himself), but with the public revival of a diehard movement among the English Unionists. They got bogged down in the intricacies of Ulster geography; which counties or which parts of Ulster might be excluded in order to satisfy the wild men? What were called those 'infernal snippets' of Tyrone and Fermanagh proved impossible to dispose of. Both men were doubly prisoners — to their principles, which they sincerely held, and to the extremists whom, they had to admit, they were powerless to control.

While these *in camera* efforts to reach a settlement were being made, some reflection of them was to be noted in public speeches. Shortly before the Leatherhead meetings, Churchill, speaking at Dundee, began on a defiant note — the Government would not allow a single Province to exercise a 'bully's veto' — but added that there were signs of a change for the better and that if only the Orangemen would moderate their language, any advance they could make would be more than matched by their Irish fellow-countrymen and the Liberals. Redmond uttered another of his little-regarded protests at this, repeating that Ireland was a unity and the two nations theory an abomination.

Liberals continued to make speeches about compromise. Reading declared himself in favour of separate and generous treatment for Ulster. The Prime Minister himself, addressing the East Fife Liberal Association at Ladybank between his first and second private meetings with Bonar Law, spoke in unusually conciliatory terms. He reasserted that at the last General Election every elector of average intelligence knew that Home Rule would be introduced, but that the Government had, even before 'the signing of Covenants and the drilling of Volunteers', been prepared to consider changes in the Bill. He made no specific promises, but his speech was generally taken as a sign of the readiness of ministers to meet the Ulster case.

Bonar Law, in the same interval between his meetings with Asquith, replied to this offer at Ladybank. He spoke again of his belief that civil war was approaching and that the country had never been in greater peril, and he pleaded yet once more for a General Election. But he was ready to consider all overtures 'when put in plain language'.

As autumn stretched into winter, it became more and more clear to those in the know that the chances of compromise were less than bright. Each side was perturbed but neither was prepared to surrender. Asquith continued to put his faith in the ultimate triumph of Parliament. The Opposition stuck to its belief that stubborn disregard for constitutional niceties would prevail in the end. And both sides solaced themselves with the reflection that their opponents were in the worse predicament. Riddell gives in his diary a glimpse of how things were moving — or rather failing to move. He met Lloyd George on the way to a Cabinet meeting, and was told that the Government policy on the Irish question had already been decided and that it was to let matters take their course and do nothing.

F. E. Smith, said Lloyd George, had been to see him and
had said that the Opposition was in serious trouble over
Ulster and did not know what to do.

The one man who remained confident was Carson, with
whom Asquith also had private talk. He found Carson
less pessimistic than the Conservative leader, but no less
adamant. Nothing short of the exclusion of Ulster would
satisfy him.

The harder the Opposition proved to bargain with, the
more plain it became to ministers that they must at least
begin to take out insurances against obstinacy in Nationalist quarters. They decided that the time had come to face
Redmond with the facts of political life as seen in the
light of the latest developments. Redmond was being a
nuisance, and must be called to heel. He wrote plaintively
to Asquith, complaining that the Ulster resistance movement had powerful enemies in its own ranks, and that they
had been gaining ground until 'the unfortunate intervention of well-intended mediators and notably the letter
of Lord Loreburn to *The Times* came to Sir Edward
Carson's rescue'. Redmond felt strongly that it was cruel
to Ireland and cruel even to the Orangemen to give
them the impression that their movement had the power
of intimidating English opinion. He sought to steady
Asquith's resolution by reminding him of 'your clear and
plain words at Ladybank' which had led the trouble-
makers to realize that 'they had to confront a minister who
would meet with firmness any overt movement on their
part'. Redmond ended by expressing his 'strongest conviction' that any offer at this moment of concessions which
he believed would bring disaster to his cause would be
calculated to give new strength and new hope to the
Orangemen.

Redmond was promptly seen by Lloyd George, who
told him that his letter had been read to the Cabinet. He
told him also that while the Cabinet was quite unanimous

in agreeing with him that to make any suggestions or proposals at the moment would be 'a fatally wrong step in tactics', the time would come when some offers would have to be made — 'sooner than we thought'. He also informed Redmond that the Government had discovered 95,000 rounds of ammunition in Belfast and that they had made up their minds at once to issue a proclamation. Redmond was assured that the Government was determined to suppress 'at any cost' armed activities in Ulster, but that when the time came for using coercive methods they would have to be accompanied by some offer to Ulster.

If no such offer were made, then Churchill, Grey and Haldane might resign, and so, Redmond recorded in his notes of the interview, 'I gathered inferentially' might Lloyd George himself. The disquieting thing about this interview, Redmond remarked, was the impression which it had left upon his mind that Lloyd George thought that in the last resort he would agree to anything rather than face the break-up of the Government. The interview had not been a propitious one, and Redmond wondered afterwards whether he had not spoken out 'more strongly and more frankly than perhaps was absolutely necessary'. But he thought, with quite unjustifiable optimism, that 'I made an impression upon him'.

The next stage in this process of softening Redmond was a soothing note to him from Asquith, repeating what Lloyd George had said about there being no question of an offer 'at this stage'. Asquith made it clear, however, that he thought it expedient to 'finish the conversation' which he had begun with Bonar Law and to 'keep our hands free, when the critical stage of the Bill is ultimately reached, to take such a course as then, in all the circumstances, seems best calculated to safeguard the fortunes of Home Rule'. Redmond carried his woes to Birrell who, as usual, was 'in the best of spirits and confident about everything'.

Redmond told him frankly what Lloyd George had said and he 'discounted a great deal — in fact most of it'. The offers on the part of the Government to sweeten the pill, which they now realized they would, sooner or later, have to make Redmond swallow, troubled them less than did what was happening in southern Ireland.

While the 'little talks', as they were referred to, between Asquith, Bonar Law and Carson were still in progress, two developments occurred in Dublin. First, Bonar Law went over there, was received enthusiastically, and made what, even for him, was an extraordinary speech. He compared Asquith's position to that of James II, who also had behind him 'the letter of the law', and who had got the judges on his side 'by methods not dissimilar from those by which Mr. Asquith got his majority in the House of Commons'. The moral drawn by Bonar Law from this historical analogy was that James II had tried to carry out his despotic intentions with the help of the largest army which had ever been seen in England. He had failed — and Asquith would do the same. Why? — because the army could refuse to fight. Here was a pretty direct appeal to the soldiers to mutiny. It had been provoked by Asquith's continued refusal to hold a General Election.

The second alarming event in Dublin followed the release, after a few weeks in prison, of Larkin. It had not failed to be noted that while his wild words had landed him at least transiently in gaol, Carson was still at large. His southern Irish supporters protested hotly against this apparent favouritism, and reminded the Liberals that they had the choice, if they were prepared to exercise it, of a wide range of Acts of Parliament under which Carson might be prosecuted. There was the Treason Felony Act of 1848, the Crimes Act of 1847 and, if these were not enough, the Unlawful Drilling Act of 1819. But they realized that the processes of the law were not going to be set in motion against any Ulster leader — and, in their hearts, they were

by no means sorry. Indeed, they had watched the growth
of militancy in the north with undisguised admiration.
It was in line with the old Irish custom of settling differences with the sister island.

Padraic Pearse — the son of a Devonshireman — who
threw himself whole-heartedly into the southern Irish
cause and was to be executed after the Easter Rising of
1916, made a comment on the Ulster Volunteers at this
time which was typical of the extremist view in the south.
'Personally', he wrote, 'I think the Orangeman with a
rifle a much less ridiculous figure than the Nationalist
without a rifle.' And he went on to wash his hands of any
suggestion that the south should take action against Ulster,
'in the present circumstances, let accursed be the soul of
any Nationalist who would dream of firing a shot or
drawing a sword against the Ulster Volunteers in connexion
with this Bill. Any such action would be an enforcement
of a British law upon the Irish populace which refused it ;
it would be a marshalling under the Union Jack.'

Those were also Larkin's sentiments, and as soon as he
was let out he called a monster meeting in Dublin for
the formation of a 'citizen army'. Thus industrial leaders
in southern Ireland had stolen a march on the political
Nationalists. The south was to resolve to have an army
bigger and better than that of Ulster — or to know the
reason why. It was puzzling to English observers — but
quite natural in Irish eyes — that Larkin had as his chief
lieutenant a Captain White, who was a Protestant Ulsterman.

The Government reacted to these growing evidences of
militancy by reimposing the ban it had lifted in the salad
days of its enjoyment of power on the import of arms
into Ireland. Two Royal Proclamations, published on
December 5, respectively prohibited the importation of arms
and ammunition into Ireland and their carriage coastwise.
Sporting guns and ammunition and explosives intended

solely for mining or other unwarlike purposes were
exempted. These Proclamations were greeted with the
comment that there were already some 80,000 rifles in
Ulster, although nobody was sure how much ammunition
there was for them. Larkin's embryo army was undoubtedly behindhand in this essential matter. But his potential
nuisance value could not be assessed. What was certain
after the failure of the Asquith-Bonar Law talks was that
the hopes of compromise had waned.

News of the talks had leaked out on December 12, but
by then they were treated rather in the manner of an
obituary notice. *The Times* emphasized that the holding
of them 'in no sense implies a truce' and, indeed, that 'it
would be rash in the highest degree to assume that such
meetings as have taken place this week are certain or even
at present likely to lead to the settlement of a problem
which has been allowed already to drift to a point of
incalculable danger'. Within a few days of the last of the
meetings, Bonar Law bearded the Liberal lions in Lloyd
George's own den. He told an audience, drawn by special
trains to Caernarvon from all parts of Wales, that the
Government was following the policy of Oliver Cromwell
by doing, not what pleased the people, but what it judged
to be for their good. He compared the treatment of Ulster
with the partition of Poland. The chances of settlement
were, he held, smaller than they had been after the Prime
Minister's Ladybank speech.

Thus the King's first patient attempt to keep the
peace had, at the close of 1913, failed. But his determination to succeed was undaunted and his influence was
to be felt again in the coming months. It was fortunate
for the country that it had in George V a monarch who
was the reverse of a Hamlet. The more the time was out
of joint, the stronger did his common sense assert itself
behind the scenes. It was to be needed, for as the Asquith-
Bonar Law negotiations failed, the professional soldiers

began to be drawn in by the civil authorities. On December 16, the date of the Asquith-Carson meeting, the Secretary of State for War, John Seely, summoned all the General Officers Commanding-in-Chief in England, Scotland and Ireland to meet him at the War Office.

SIR SPENCER EWART AND FIELD-MARSHAL SIR JOHN FRENCH

CHAPTER VIII

ENTER THE GENERALS

SEVERAL of the senior officers who attended the meeting at the War Office were remarkable personalities, and none was more so than the Secretary of State for War. Seely (later Lord Mottistone) was one of those men around whom legend and anecdote cluster thick in lifetime. He came of good Liberal stock. His grandfather, who sat for many years as Liberal member for Lincoln, had invited Garibaldi to England in the 'sixties, and had upset Queen Victoria by his uninhibited radicalism. On the occasion of her first Jubilee she had visited the Isle of Wight, where the Seelys were prominent landowners. She had reminded him of the past and, bowing to her as she sat in her carriage, he had said, 'Well, Ma'am, I suppose that as we get older we get wiser'. The grandson could scarcely have made that claim — nor would he have wanted to do so.

His flair was for action, often gallant and sometimes ill advised. He had served with distinction as a yeomanry officer in the Anglo-Boer war, getting out to South Africa by a display of characteristic enterprise. There had been some difficulties about finding a ship for the yeomanry, and Captain Seely had applied to his uncle, who was Chairman of the Union Castle Line, asking him: 'Uncle Frank, have you got a spare ship?' Sir Francis Evans had one. — 'Then I want it,' said the nephew. 'Who is going to pay for it?' asked the uncle. 'Never mind about that. If you produce a ship, the War Office is bound to pay.' The War Office grumbled that it was 'a most odd and irregular proceeding' but, thanks to his friendship with Wolseley, Seely got his way.

He entered Parliament as a Conservative with the laurels of the South African campaign on him, and he quickly got caught up among the young Conservatives who, to the delight of Rosebery and other Liberal connoisseurs of skilful parliamentary sniping, proceeded to make the lives of Balfour's ministers in general, and of his Secretary of State for War in particular, miserable. It was not long before this impatience with the old 'Hotel Cecil' brand of Toryism, combining with his radical background, induced Seely to cross the floor of the House As a child he had sat on John Bright's knee; as a Harrow schoolboy he had had tea with Gladstone, and both his grandfathers had been forceful members of the Anti-Corn Law League. Dislike of Chamberlain's attempt to force Tariff Reform on the Conservative Party was thus another motive for the change of allegiance. Seely took up the Liberal cause, including the attack on Chinese labour in the gold mines, with gusto, and he was disappointed not immediately to be given office.

He kept his friends on both sides of the House throughout life. Who could fail to be fond of a man who could tell, as Seely did, so many stories against himself? He once recalled that he related to Balfour the details of a nasty accident he had suffered in Switzerland, which had laid him up with concussion of the brain for many months. Balfour, 'turning to me with his benevolent smile, said slowly, "My dear Jack, that explains it all!" Perhaps it does!' A *beau sabreur*, excelling as a rider to hounds, as a cliff-climber and as a sailor, Seely was always at his happiest in rough water. The French Government gave him a gold medal for a swim of extraordinary bravery which he undertook to carry a line to a ship in distress.

Truth such as this was often mixed with fable in the anecdotes of which he was the hero. F. E. Smith said that

Jack (he was Jack to all his friends) had once seen a man struggling in an angry sea. A small crowd was watching from the end of a pier, but no one dared to dive in to the rescue. Seely promptly did so, and a violent struggle followed. The struggling man was saved, but had in the process to be stunned. On coming out, Seely remarked, 'That was the most troublesome man whose life I have ever saved.' He then learned that he had saved the champion swimmer of the south of England, who was giving an exhibition of life-saving.

The apocrypha of the War Office includes the story of an early Labour War Minister who, on being asked to sanction the movement of a brigade in Palestine, replied, 'Its no use coming to me, lad, I'm a pacifist'. The shortest definition of Seely is the negative one that he was the opposite of this mythical successor in his office. He took war-like decisions with equal gusto and lack of wisdom.

The transition from Haldane to Seely was abrupt for the soldiers. They found that they had exchanged a Schopenhauer, of whom they had first been scared and had then grown to like, for a Cyrano de Bergerac. But they were accustomed to having, through the exigencies of Cabinet reshufflings, unexpected individuals at their head. The best that the Liberals had given them, within living memory at that time, were the two highly civilian Scots, Campbell-Bannerman and Haldane. Seely's outstanding record on active service won him their respect but not, in all cases, either their affection or their confidence. The least sensitive among them was well aware that the army was going through revolutionary changes. European war was more than a possibility in the foreground of their calculations. The South African war, in which most of them had fought, was a vivid and, in many respects, a painful memory.

The soldier best known to the general public was no longer at their head, but his extremely lively little shadow

still cast its shape across their deliberations. Roberts had
been made Commander-in-Chief on the strength of his
success in South Africa. It had been an unhappy appointment, and, as soon as decently possible, he had been
removed and his office had been at long last abolished. An
Army Council had replaced a Commander-in-Chief. The
change had not, however, eclipsed Roberts. He continued to be a well-publicized advocate of conscription and,
as has been seen earlier in these pages, he had put his
influence actively at the disposal of the Ulster Volunteers.

This latter activity of his neither surprised nor disturbed
high-ranking officers over whose collective shoulders his
mantle had been thrown, but there was one view which he
held that was still regarded as objectionably heretical by
some of them. His experience in South Africa and earlier
in the field had so impressed him with the growing
efficiency of fire-power that he had come to doubt whether
cavalry any longer could efficiently carry out its traditional
and cherished role of charging with cold steel. He had
embodied these new notions of how mounted troops might
be best employed in the *Manual of Cavalry Training*,
which was in the course of preparation during his last
years at the War Office. Happily, from the point of view
of the generals (most of them cavalrymen) who disagreed
with him, his retirement had strategically been arranged
before this official text-book appeared.

It never would have appeared had he not protested
from his retirement. 'Although I have submitted to great
discourtesy', he wrote, 'while the recent changes at the
War Office have been carried out, when it only affected me
personally, I cannot consent to submit to it when it involves
action which, in my opinion, is detrimental to the Service.'
The dispute around the *Manual*, which was first issued
provisionally for six months, and then put into general
military circulation without its preface, to which Roberts
attached great importance, flickered on for some time.

Roberts continued to harass the orthodox cavalry soldiers. He wrote a foreword to *War and the Arme Blanche*, a study of cavalry tactics published in 1910. Its author, Erskine Childers (best known to British readers for *The Riddle of the Sands*), was to fight against Britain in the Sinn Fein cause and to be executed as a rebel by the Irish Free State Government. The permutations of fortune among individuals involved in Anglo-Irish affairs were incalculable. When Roberts supported Erskine Childers's tactical theories, he argued that the 'cavalry spirit' was the same as that by which engineers were inspired to blow open the gates of a walled city.

Sir John French, who, at the date of the December War Office meeting, was Chief of the Imperial General Staff, held strong views in conflict with those of Roberts. Nothing, he had told Roberts, 'can make me alter the view that I hold on the subject of cavalry'. The most he was prepared to consider was that there should be some minor changes in equipment. 'My idea is', he had declared, 'that Hussars and Lancers should retain all the arms they now carry, but that the lances should be taken away from Dragoon Guards and Dragoons, who should be armed like Hussars.' And he had put himself on record as 'strongly arguing the necessity for getting a better sword'. He had noted with irritation the gibes of civilians at the time of the Anglo-Boer war. H. H. Munro (Saki) had made the then Secretary of State for War, Lansdowne, lament that the Boers were no mortal foes, they were mounted infantry. Any suggestion that British cavalry should be made more like mounted infantry disturbed French.

He was an old Hussar who had entered the army, after a brief and unsatisfactory experience as a midshipman in the 'sixties, through the Militia. He had avoided Sandhurst. His interests were not political, and he had been too much occupied in keeping the flag of professional military conservatism flying in army training to concern himself with the repercussions of the raising of the Ulster Volunteers. He was well aware that trouble was brewing, but had not devoted any systematic thought to its possible effects on the army. But he was, within three months, to be dragged into the centre of the whirlpool.

So was the Adjutant-General, Sir Spencer Ewart, who was also present at Seely's meeting. He came of an ancient Scottish family, and had served in the Cameron Highlanders, going to the War Office immediately after doing well in South Africa. He was aware that some officers were worried about what they might be called upon to do in Ireland. Sir Wyndham Childs, a staff captain in the Disciplinary Branch of the War Office in 1914, had been asked by Ewart what the young officers were thinking. Childs had told him that so long as he held His Majesty's commission he did not intend to consider the position until matters reached the breaking-point. Ewart asked him what he called the breaking-point. He replied that it was the movement of the rifle from the 'ready' to the 'present'.

Many such informal conversations had been held on the eve of the Seely meeting, and no one had thrown himself into them with more relish than had the Director of Military Operations, Sir Henry Wilson. Legend had delighted to busy herself with this remarkable individual, almost as much as with Seely. His handsome figure, moving restlessly from the soldiers to the politicians, was well known in Westminster. It was said of him that he was the greatest intriguer who had ever worn the King's uniform.

He was an Irishman whose family had gone over with William III and acquired land in Antrim. At first it had not seemed certain that he would be able to make the army his career. He failed twice to get into Woolwich and three times to get into Sandhurst — no mean feat. The convenient back door of the Militia let him in as it had French.

The Longford Militia and the Royal Irish Regiment saw
him transiently, and then, in the 'eighties, he was gazetted
into the Rifle Brigade. It was a foot regiment but, like its
comrades of the 60th, well able to look the cavalry in the
face — look over their heads, as riflemen would put it.
Churchill's father had proposed that he should enter the
Rifles, but the competition for the infantry was keener as
life in the cavalry was so much more expensive. Once
Wilson had got into this crack regiment, he never looked
back. He had a flair for impressing influential people.
Roberts first met him at a cricket match in the 'nineties
and helped him to prosper in the South African campaign.

Within ten years of joining the Rifle Brigade, he was
installed in the Intelligence Department of the War Office,
at the head of which was his Irish friend, Sir John Ardagh.
A little later he made a name for himself as a lecturer at
the Staff College. As a public speaker he was fluent. His
command of idiom, humorous, pungent and delightfully
indiscreet, pleased a wider public than that of the students
of the Staff College. Foch, whom he met in the course of
the military talks with France, found him a refreshing
exception to the average run of British officers. This
friendship between the Irish and French soldiers lasted
until the former was murdered. But that was after the
First World War and a long time ahead. Foch wrote of
Wilson that 'Au contact de sa nature chaude, droite,
franche, et, par-dessus tout, désintéressée, il était facile de
travailler en parfait accord avec lui, et, si l'on ne partageait
pas entièrement son sentiment sur certaines manières
d'agir ou de penser, on n'en restait pas moins plein d'estime
et d'attachement pour l'homme'.

The nuances of this tribute were beginning to make
themselves known to British politicians and soldiers in
1914. Many of them had found his nature attractive,
though few of them would have described him as dis-
interested, and all would have agreed that they did not

entirely share his ideas of how to set about things.

In December 1913 he had just been gazetted Major-General, having risen from the rank of Captain in twelve years, which was good going in time of peace. He had already had reason to differ with Seely over Ulster and other matters. A lecture he had given at the University of London on frontiers had caused Seely to take umbrage and to send for him. Wilson recorded the interview in his diary, which was subsequently to be published and to provoke no little stir in the 'twenties. The Secretary of State for War, he wrote, 'tried to check me for my lecture yesterday, but I wasn't for it'.

This brush with a Cabinet minister of a political party to which Wilson did not belong was merely incidental to his other preoccupations. He had had some frank talks with French in November. French had asked him what he thought about Ulster. 'I told him that I could not fire on the North at the dictation of Redmond, and this is what the whole thing means. England *qua* England is opposed to Home Rule, and England must agree to it before it is carried out. . . . I *cannot* bring myself to believe that Asquith will be so mad as to employ force. It will split the army and the Colonies, as well as the country and the Empire.'

A few days after this discussion he advised French 'to put in writing the fact that he could not be responsible for the whole of the army. This Ulster business is getting serious.' But Wilson did not confine himself in airing his views on Ireland to listeners in his own service. He was hand-in-glove with the Conservative politicians. Civil servants at the War Office observed with raised eyebrows that the telephone of the Director of Military Operations was often liable to put him in touch, during office hours, with Bonar Law and other politicians. Bonar Law found Wilson a valuable and an encouraging source of information on the state of opinion in the army.

SIR JOHN SEELY

SIR HENRY WILSON

From the portrait by Birley at Marlborough College

'I told him', Wilson wrote of one of his visits to Bonar
Law, 'that there was much talk in the army, and that if
we were ordered to coerce Ulster there would be wholesale
defections. It had been suggested to him that 40 per cent
of officers and men would leave the army. Personally I put
the pc. much lower, but still very serious. I then told him
of Cecil's idea that Carson should pledge the Ulster troops
to fight for England if she was at war. I pointed out that
a move like this would render the employment of troops
against Ulster more impossible than ever. He was much
pleased with the suggestion and at once tried to get Carson
on the telephone. He was, however, away for the day.
Bonar Law will see him tomorrow.

'I then told B. L. of my coming evidence before the
C.I.D. Invasion Committee, and how I proposed to tackle
the subject with my problems. He entirely agreed. We
then discussed the Linlithgow and Reading elections.
Asquith was going to approach B. L. with a proposal to
exclude the four Northern Counties. This, of course,
wrecks the present Bill, and puts B. L. into an awkward
position, as Ulster won't agree; and then Asquith can
exclaim intolerance. On the other hand, Asquith is in a
much tighter place, because Johnnie Redmond and Devlin
can't agree to the exclusion of Ulster. The thing to do,
therefore, is to make Redmond wreck the proposal. This,
and much more talk of a confidential nature, made my
morning very interesting. B. L. realizes what a difficult
place he is in with tariff reform and food taxes. But on the
whole his prospects are much more rosy than Asquith's.'

Bonar Law was not the only civilian contact of this
highly political general. As the day of the Seely meeting
approached, the Director of Military Operations led a busy
social life. He lunched with Milner at Brooks's and learned
from that stern unbending Tory proconsul several things
to his advantage. The Unionists of England, Milner told
him — in the historic Whig house where Charles Fox had

once gambled and praised the French Revolution — would
soon have to pass from words to deeds. One of their first
declarations would be to make clear that, if any officers
resigned, they would be reinstated when the Conservatives
came into power. 'I was glad', Wilson confided in his
diary, 'to hear all this.'

He was no less glad to hear at lunch on the following
day how the arrangements for defying the constitution
were progressing in Ulster. One of the 'Five', as he called
them, who were planning this Ulster campaign, Edward
Sclater, was 'most interesting'. Wilson gave him some
advice; the Volunteers had better avoid such 'pitfalls'
as the seizure of arms depots; the army was becoming
most sympathetic to the Ulster movement and it would
look well if the readiness of the Ulstermen to come over
and help England if she got into trouble were stressed.

Every turn in the affair was followed by Wilson with
keen and partisan attention. He approved the theory that,
if hostilities did break out, England would have to grant
belligerent rights to Ulster as the Federals had done to the
Confederates in the American Civil War, and he was
disappointed when Lord Halsbury brought the formidable
weight of his legal authority down on the other side. He
favoured a suggestion that all Unionists in the Territorials
should resign. It was natural that a general who mixed
himself up so openly and so uninhibitedly in politics
should have been regarded with suspicion at the time and
in later years and that his share in what happened has been
stressed. But he did not hold a key position; his influence,
of which more will be said as the troubles developed, was
rather that of a father confessor in anti-governmental circles
than of an active director of civil war operations.

One of his comrades who came over at the summons
of the War Minister was, through no wish of his own, to
be forced to play an active and a disastrous part. Arthur
Henry Fitzroy Paget commanded the troops in Ireland.

His military service stretched back to the late 'sixties; he had done well under Wolseley in the Ashanti War in the 'seventies and again at Suakim. He narrowly escaped having to retire on grounds of seniority in the 'nineties; but the fates were kind to him and he just got promoted in time to take over the Scots Guards, and so was able to go out to South Africa where he commanded a brigade. Trouble with his superiors led to his return, although the Prince of Wales brought influence to bear on keeping him in the field.

He was 'Artie' to the Prince of Wales whose man-of-the-worldly avocations he shared, at home and in Paris, before and after Edward came to the throne. His family connections with royalty were of long standing. He had been a Page of Honour to Queen Victoria, and his father Equerry and Clerk Marshal of the Household. His grandfather, the first Marquis of Anglesey, had (while still Earl of Uxbridge) lost a leg at Waterloo and, later, as Lord-Lieutenant, had provoked O'Connell to wish 'that ridiculously self-conceited Lord Anglesey were out of Ireland; I take him to be our greatest enemy'. Living to a ripe old age he became a well-known social figure. It is he, rather than the Duke of Wellington, who was credited, in Victorian anecdotage, with having cheered Queen Caroline, when forced to do so by a mob of her sympathizers, and then exclaimed, 'The Queen — may all your wives be like her!'

His grandson was a chip of the old block around whom stories collected almost as thickly as they did around Seely. Sir Arthur Paget's gallantry in the field was recognized, but he was not widely regarded as cool or clear-headed. The flash-point at which his temper burst into flames was low in the scale. An air of unaffected arrogance clung to him. His conversation was said to be interlarded with such remarks as 'so I massed a hundred guns' and 'then I launched my Guards'. He claimed to 'live history rather than to read it'; he had hobbies other than reading. When he died in 1928 his obituary notice in *The Times*, evidently written in a friendly spirit, included as back-handed a compliment as can ever have been paid to a deceased general: 'Had he only devoted to military study', the obituarist reflected, 'a fraction of the time which he gave up to the observation of trees and shrubs, he might have ranked as a learned soldier'.

Such were the generals and such was the Cabinet Minister at their head when the Conference met at the War Office on December 16, 1913. Seely opened proceedings by telling them what they already well knew, that he had received news that certain officers proposed to resign their commissions rather than to carry out any order to attack Ulster. He then made a statement which he subsequently published. These are his words:

'I first deal with the legal question. The law clearly lays down that a soldier is entitled to obey an order to shoot only if that order is reasonable under the circumstances. No one, from general officer to private, is entitled to use more force than is required to maintain order and the safety of life and property. No soldier can shelter himself from the civil law behind an order given by a superior if that order is, in fact, unreasonable and outrageous.

'If therefore, officers and men in the Army are led to believe that there was a possibility that they might be called upon to take some outrageous action, for instance, to massacre a demonstration of Orangemen who were causing no danger to the lives of their neighbours, bad as might be the effects on discipline in the Army, nevertheless, it is true that they are, in fact and in law, justified in contemplating refusal to obey.

'But there never has been, and is not now, any intention of giving outrageous and illegal orders to the troops. The law will be respected and must be obeyed. What has now to be faced is the possibility of action being required by

His Majesty's troops in supporting the civil power, in protecting life and property if the police are unable to hold their own.

'Attempts have been made to dissuade troops from obeying lawful orders given to them when acting in support of the Civil Power. This amounts to a claim that officers and men can pick and choose between lawful and reasonable orders, saying that they will obey in one case and not in another.

'The Army has been quite steady. During the past year there has not been brought to the notice of the authorities one single case of lack of discipline in this respect. At the same time, in view of the statements in the Press and elsewhere, it is well to make the position clear.'

The ambiguities in that appreciation were as plain to those who heard it as were its disquieting possibilities. How could a soldier be sure that an order to shoot was or was not 'reasonable under the circumstances'? When the military are brought in to support the civil power, circumstances may alter at bewildering speed — and not least in Ireland. Where would 'the possibility of action' lead them? If they obeyed an order that was afterwards ruled to have been 'unreasonable', they would be in trouble. But they were forbidden to 'pick and choose'. Paget could no more follow these instructions than he could have made a précis of the Athanasian Creed.

But he and the other generals were directed by Seely to 'make the position thus outlined perfectly clear to all concerned', and they were warned that he would 'hold each of them individually responsible to see that there was no conduct in their commands subversive to discipline'. If there were, it would be dealt with forthwith under the King's Regulations. An officer who sent in his resignation must be asked why he did so and, if he answered that he contemplated refusing to obey a lawful order, Seely would at once 'submit to the King that the officer should be removed'.

On this perplexing note the Conference closed and the generals dispersed to their commands. While they were in London, they had heard more of how things were shaping than they got from their political chief. They took back with them some glimpses of the other side of the hill which Wilson was so well able to supply. And, whichever way they looked, they did not like it. One of the senior officers at the War Office has summed up how they all felt.

Sir Nevil Macready, Director of Personal Services, had had more experience than any of them of the perils by which a soldier may be encompassed in time of civil war. Macready's past was now finding him out; Seely was sending him to and from Ireland to report on the situation because he had made a reputation for himself in the recent strikes in South Wales and Lancashire. It was not a duty that he relished; as became the son of a great actor, he knew how to gauge the mood of a crowd and the gift had proved invaluable at Pontypridd and in Salford. There had been no question, on the occasion of those strikes, of officers sending in their papers. But the task of keeping order while strikes were on had been none the less dis-agreeable.

Churchill, as Home Secretary, had, so Macready complained, packed him off 'in his usual impetuous way' to the Welsh Valleys and, then, when he got there, 'could not refrain from telling me where I ought to sleep'. Once Macready had had time to take stock of the situation on the spot, he found Churchill a chief who backed him in the face of much political and press criticism. All went well, in that no serious clashes occurred between the troops and the strikers. But the recent memory of this appeal by the civil power to the army was the reverse of encouraging and what Seely had said confirmed the worst professional military forebodings.

As Macready put it, 'to be responsible for troops and police when engaged in the suppression of disorder is one of the most trying and disagreeable duties a soldier can be called upon to perform. The least slip on the part of a subordinate may turn the scale, or political pressure may demand a scapegoat.' He recalled that not even the clarity of a Haldane could simplify this dark, explosive question. The one thing of which a general could be sure was 'whatever you do, you are sure to regret it'. So they all agreed. But, as they waited for the politicians to make a last effort to avoid the worst, they hoped that no call would reach them. All the loose talk of resignations and refusals to march was as repugnant to the average regular officer, of high rank or low, as it was to Spender himself.

Suspicion of an organized army 'plot', of which much was to be heard in the coming months, had no truth behind it. The consequence of the Seely meeting was that the confusion of mind into which most of the civilian leaders of the nation had plunged themselves infected some of the military leaders. The latter were to have an uneasy breathing-space while, for the next three months, the Ministry sought to reach an eleventh-hour agreement with its unyielding opponents. How this was done on the floor of the House and how it was supplemented by activities behind the scenes are subjects that carry the narrative nearly to the end of the first quarter of 1914.

CHAPTER IX

THE PLOT IS HATCHED

EARLY in the New Year of 1914 the King sought, once again, to influence his Prime Minister without overstepping the bounds of constitutional propriety. He repeated to Asquith at Windsor what was by now, to him and to others, the commonplace that many army officers would send in their papers rather than fight. 'But whom are they going to fight?' Asquith placidly asked in reply. It was a question that might have been differently put. If no one was going to fight anybody, then why had the Government alerted the army commanders and why were the Ulster Volunteers drilling, day and night? The evidence that they were doing so, in the highest spirits and with the greatest efficiency, came in from all sides.

Carson had been inspecting their regiments in January as though he were a military man and not what Birrell had just called him — an 'elderly barrister'. He had warned a post-prandial gathering in Belfast that Churchill had told him, a week or so earlier, that 'he would fight it out'. The Ulstermen were ready for the fight. Their strength, by the turn of the year, was coming up to 100,000; the fund to indemnify them against the losses of civil war had passed its £1,000,000 mark; their zeal in training was said to compare favourably with that of Territorials, preparing for nothing more serious than a possible war against Germany.

An atmosphere of gravity oppressed the nation. The Archbishop of York, preaching on the text 'Blessed are the Peacemakers', urged that something must be done to prevent a civil war. But the peacemakers were not conspicuous across the water. 'Wherever one went one found organization and drill in hand', Gleichen noted from his brigade headquarters in Ulster. 'The large landowners, almost to a man Unionists, and many of them ex-officers of the Regulars or late Militia, peers and commoners, rich men or well-to-do farmers, held local meetings and enrolled nearly all their men in the Volunteer force. They went round their properties night after night, superintending the organization and attending at the drill halls to see that all was going well. Some had given up their parks to batches of men for a week or more's training at a time. The wife of one of the big owners told me at the end of 1913 that for the last two or three months she had not seen her husband except on Sundays, and that night after night he returned exhausted from his rounds.'

Wilson slipped over to Ulster in January and returned full of admiration for the discipline and spirit of the Volunteers and with a fund of 'many remarkable stories of Carson's power'. It had to be a brief visit, but he expressed the resolve to go again and 'see the troops at work'. The troops of the army in which he himself served saw comparatively little of him on this occasion. He was very secretive and spent much time closeted with the Unionist leaders. What he learned he carried back to Bonar Law and other recipients of his confidence in the Opposition ranks.

The Government, too, had its agents at work in Ulster and the reports they produced grew more and more disturbing. What precisely they amounted to is hard to disentangle — for what was later made public lacks consistency. Macready, who had first been sent over by Seely to explore the ground in the previous autumn, drew an emphatic picture of sinister activities. He declared that the Volunteers were, by the turn of the year, seeking information about the strength of the Royal Irish

I

Constabulary and coastguards, the staffs of post offices and railway stations and the halls and meeting-places of two Roman Catholic bodies, the Ancient Order of Hibernians and the United Irish League.

Did this mean that the Volunteers were contemplating some *coup d'état* or were they merely concerned to gun-run on an ambitious scale, so as to be prepared for any contingency? The Government did not know what to think; but, week by week, its nerves, or at least those of some ministers, got more and more on edge. Seely, acting on rumours that Carrickfergus Castle might be attacked, asked Churchill, in January, to let him have a ship to protect it. The request was refused and this old Norman castle on Belfast Lough, where some 85 tons of army ammunition were stored, remained without extra guard until mid-March.

But Seely, apprehensive though he was of attacks on Carrickfergus and other places where arms were kept, acquitted 'Carson and any responsible leader' of being aware of such plans. Who was to carry them out, if not the Volunteers, remained a doubtful point. Belief in their reality gathered force as spring approached, for 'evil-disposed persons' — the phrase is Churchill's — were only too likely to appear unexpectedly on the Ulster scene.

The sceptical Gleichen cast doubt on these rumours. Neither he nor the police, he asserted, knew anything about them 'and our intelligence was rather good'. But he cautiously added 'we were after all not omniscient'. It was a sensible postscript; for no one can claim omniscience in searching for a needle in a haystack, and that is what intelligence designed to get to the bottom of Irish troubles, real or imaginary, amounted to in practice. Certain reality was bad enough to give any Government reason to worry. The Volunteers now had machine-guns, aeroplanes and ambulances and had worked out how best to break down railways and employ light columns against an 'enemy'.

The Ulster ladies were in the thick of it, as nurses and signallers and on telegraphic and postal duties. English ladies were helping them by preparing their homes to receive refugee 'loyalists' — a useful dress rehearsal, so it turned out, for the advent, later in 1914, of Belgians escaping from the Kaiser's occupation of their country.

An extra stroke of shadow was painted into this already dark picture by the attitude of the Royal Irish Constabulary. Macready was sorry to be obliged to come to the conclusion that 'this once magnificent body of men had undoubtedly deteriorated to what was almost a state of supine lethargy and had lost even the semblance of energy or initiative when a crisis demanded vigorous and resolute action'. *Quis custodiet ipsos custodes?* Only the Volunteers had the answer to that speculation. Every week that passed made it more and more undeniable that, as soon as the Home Rule Act had received the King's Consent, Carson's army and civil service would take over the maintenance of law and order and of administration generally in the Northern Counties. Nothing short of force would stop them. Resort to force would be a perilous adventure, and yet, what was the alternative? Asquith tried desperately to find it by consent. This involved him and his ministerial colleagues in two parallel sets of negotiations which went on into March.

He approached Carson yet again, only having, on January 22, to tell the Cabinet that he met with a 'flat refusal' of anything short of the exclusion of Ulster. Still he did not lose hope. If Carson was adamant as a rock, another imprint could be left on the shifting sands of the Nationalist Party. Redmond, who had had no direct dealings with the Cabinet since November, was summoned, on February 2, to an interview with the Prime Minister. He was told of the repeated 'little talks' between Asquith, Bonar Law and Carson and that 'these gentlemen maintained their position obstinately'. Ministers, Asquith

assured him, had no wish to exclude Ulster — even
temporarily. But they now feared a crisis over the Army
Annual Bill. If that did not get passed in March or April,
the Army would legally be disbanded. The Opposition
were, so Asquith had reason to believe, ripe for mischief
and likely to cause yet another disturbance in the House,
holding up business and with it the passage of the Army
Bill.

The meeting lasted an hour and a half, with Birrell,
who was there, saying, for once, 'practically nothing'. It
left Redmond afraid that the King was bringing strong
pressure on the Prime Minister and uncertain how far the
Cabinet meant to go in making an inevitable 'offer to
Ulster'. He did not have long to wait. Devlin vainly
endeavoured to come to the aid of his chief with a lengthy
and eloquent memorandum to which Lloyd George replied.
There were more meetings between Redmond, Dillon,
Devlin, Lloyd George and Birrell, and then, on March 2,
again with Asquith. On the same day, Asquith wrote to
Carson inviting him, 'in consequence of something which
the King said to me', to see him once more at 'our old
trysting place, 24 Queen Anne's Gate'.

But Carson was in no yielding mood. His was the
happy position of counsel, quite certain of the verdict
being in his favour, listening to appeals from the other side
for a settlement out of court. Two days before he kept
the fruitless tryst with Asquith he had received an agreeable
letter from Milner. It told him of a declaration, in
support of the Ulster Convention, which had been signed,
among others, by Roberts, Kipling, Professor Dicey, the
Dean of Canterbury, the Duke of Portland, Lord Des-
borough, Lord Lovat and Admiral Seymour — and
signatures were still rolling in.

At last, on March 9, the Government faced the House
with a revised version of Home Rule which had been
forced, as the last limits of concession, on a majority of the

reluctant, resentful and apprehensive Nationalists and that might — or might not — satisfy the Ulster leaders and their Conservative allies.

Competition for tickets had been keen and the House was packed to overflowing. Lucky strangers filled the high galleries. The two small galleries below, on the Speaker's right for the Lords and on the left for distinguished visitors, held an eminent crush. On the floor of the House members sat tightly wedged together on the benches and the steps of the gangway, or stood in a knot at the Bar or squeezed themselves, sitting or standing, into the side galleries. Asquith, coming in at Question Time, took his seat on the Treasury Bench between Lloyd George and Birrell. He was loudly cheered by the Liberals and received in silence by the Nationalists. Bonar Law and Carson, entering together, aroused a roar of welcome from the Opposition.

At a quarter to four the first order of the day, 'Government of Ireland Bill — Second Reading', was read by the Clerk. Asquith, looking unembarrassed and confident, rose. As he did so, it was noted that he was laughing at a remark made in his ear by the irrepressible Birrell. 'Our proposals', Asquith said, 'are put forward as the price of peace'. They showed, indeed, a momentous change of policy and one that was a direct contradiction of what ministers had so repeatedly defended in public for the past two years. The counties of Ulster, including the county boroughs of Belfast and Londonderry, were to be allowed to contract out of Home Rule by a bare majority vote. But, six years after the meeting of the Irish Parliament, any county which had, in this way, gained temporary exclusion would automatically come into the scheme of that Parliament. The interval must include two general elections, so that the electorate in both countries would have ample experience of the working of the Irish executive. Unwilling counties could not be forced in unless with the assent of a majority of voters in the whole British Isles. The arrangement was, he affirmed, 'fair and equitable'.

The House was not kept in suspense as to how this 'last word' appealed to Bonar Law and Carson. Promptly the former denounced the offer; it left matters, he protested, very grave indeed. Redmond followed to say that, if the Government offer were frankly accepted by the Unionists 'as the basis of agreement and peace' he would acquiesce. But it was a sacrifice and, if it were rejected, the Government's duty must be to employ 'all the resources at its command' to suppress any movement that might arise to overawe Parliament or subvert the law by the menace of force. His followers received this with a wild cheer. The Unionists joined in with a fierce cry that sounded as a challenge to battle.

O'Brien came next, lamenting the dismemberment of Ireland into 'a thing of shreds and patches'. Then there was a hush as Carson rose, succeeded by sympathetic cheers. He had been ill and had not been certainly expected in his place. His voice was laboured but his words left — for clarity — nothing to be desired. 'We do not want', he told the House, 'sentence of death with a stay of execution for six years.' It was a whip-lash across the face of the ministers who had so patiently been wooing him. Carson rounded on Redmond. 'The Hon. and learned member for Waterford said that if these proposals were rejected the path of duty for the majority in this House is clear. They must assert their authority, they must go straight through with the Bill and they must employ all the resources of the Government to enforce it against his Ulster fellow countrymen.'

'Well, Sir,' Carson proceeded, 'that may be the duty of the House. Men talk very lightly about the enforcement of any law. I know something about the difficulty. You may make up your minds to do that, but if there is a duty upon the part of the Government there is also a duty upon the part of the country and I appeal from the Government to the country. I say to the country, "Are you going to allow the forces of the Crown, which are your forces and not the forces of any political caucus, to be used to coerce men who have asked nothing but that they should remain with you?' And if you are, are you going to give up, even for a moment, to a Government which may be here today and gone tomorrow, the right yourselves to determine what is real liberty, and this to a Government who have refused, when asked, to appeal to the country?"'

This was a declaration of war and as such the Cabinet received it. At the cost of straining the loyalty of the Nationalists to breaking point — in some cases beyond it — nothing had been gained. The hopes expressed so recently that if an offer of temporary exclusion were rejected it would 'put the other side entirely in the wrong' (as Lloyd George had prophesied) proved to be dupes. Public opinion reacted no more unfavourably to Carson's defiant speech than it had to previous assertions of Ulster's will to resist. Unless something were done to reassert the authority of the Government, its writ would cease to run in the Northern Counties.

Alarm and despondency in governmental circles had just been still further spread by a renewal of the rumours that mischief was brewing in Ulster. Intelligence reports, that did not come from the military on the spot, suggested that the evil-disposed persons were plotting to raid the stores of arms and ammunition at Armagh, Omagh, Enniskillen and, yet again, Carrickfergus. Asquith had been sufficiently impressed by these reports to sanction the setting up, a few days before the debate of March 9, of a special Cabinet committee. Its function was to consider what should be done to frustrate the alleged plotters and to report, without delay, to the Cabinet.

The members of this committee were Crewe, Birrell, Churchill and Seely. Crewe was to take the chair and to exercise the moderating influence of an elder statesman on his two more impetuous colleagues. Birrell was there, of course, because he always had to be, *ex officio*, when Irish affairs were under discussion. The sad fate of the concessions offered in the House caused this committee to be galvanized into dramatic activity. The patience of Churchill and Seely was exhausted. They were men of action and, as their ex-Tory associates had gone about Ulster encouraging the Volunteers, they had detested the role of restraint which had been forced upon them. Now, like Job's war-horse and a stable companion, they smelt battle afar off.

They would forestall any attempt on the part of the Ulstermen to go into action. Two could play at soldiers and, after all, the lawful army and navy were behind them. By an accidental stroke of fate, the moderating presence of Crewe was temporarily withdrawn. As the ministers of the fighting services went ahead at full speed with their preparations, Crewe fell sick after a dinner at the Savoy, on the evening of March 12, where he had been the principal guest of the Institution of Mining and Metallurgy. The indisposition was temporary but critical in its consequences.

March 12 was a Thursday. Two days later, Cubitt, Secretary of the Army Council, sent a letter from the War Office to Paget. Cubitt conveyed to the old general the commands of the Army Council. They were that special precautions should be taken at once for safeguarding depots and other places where arms or stores were kept 'as you may think advisable'. Officers in command of all barracks where guns, small arms and ammunition were located must be warned that they would be held responsible for the safety of these stores. Several danger spots were specifically listed, but Paget was not left to confine himself to them. His orders required him 'to ensure the safety of Government arms and stores in the south as well as in the north of Ireland'.

While this letter was on its way, Churchill was travelling up to Bradford, where he delivered a pugnacious speech. The Prime Minister, he said, had made a fair and responsible offer which represented the hardest sacrifice ever asked of Irish nationalism and which was a final offer. But the Unionists still showed the old spirit of ascendancy. They seemed to think that a settlement could only be achieved by threats. Well, in the event of violence the larger issue would be dominant. Was parliamentary government to be broken down before the menace of armed force ? That had been fought out at Marston Moor. Apparently some sections of the propertied class desired to subvert parliamentary government. Against such a mood, when manifested in action, there was no legal measure from which the Government could or would shrink. He had had to send soldiers out during the railway strike, and there was no Unionist condemnation then ; Great Britain must not be reduced to the condition of Mexico. If the British civil and parliamentary systems were to be brought to the challenge of force, he could only say — and his words were to go echoing through the weeks and months ahead — 'let us go forward together and put these grave matters to the proof'.

The pudding thus to be put to the proof was, for the moment, being stirred by the agitated hands of Paget ; his chief in London did not feel quite happy that they were the right hands. On Monday, March 16, Seely telegraphed to Paget, instructing him to reply by wire 'not later than 8 A.M. tomorrow' what he had done about the Cubitt letter. The same telegram summoned Paget to be at the War Office at 10.45 A.M. on Wednesday, 'bringing with you full plans in detail'. Paget replied that he had issued 'general instructions' and had taken 'all available steps'. He would send details next day by post.

The House met as these messages were going to and from Ireland. Churchill, on the strength of his Bradford speech, was greeted with cheers that did not, at that time, often come to him from the Liberal benches. He received too, from Asquith, an emphatic endorsement of what he had said. The Liberal temper was stiff and confident.

On Tuesday, March 17, Paget wrote his promised letter. He explained in it that two of the places specifically entrusted to his care were being guarded, and that steps were being taken to remove reserve arms from the other two places. The operation would take about a week. Paget was nervous about the wisdom of embarking upon troop movements: 'In the present state of the country, I am of the opinion that any such movement of troops would create intense excitement in Ulster, and possibly precipitate a crisis. For these reasons I do not consider myself justified in moving troops at the present time, although I am keeping a sufficient number in readiness to move at short notice in case the situation should develop into a more dangerous state.' A final, plaintive paragraph drew attention to the fact that 'there is no Intelligence Service in this command; and that all the reliable political information is received by me at second-hand, so that I am placed at a considerable disadvantage in attempting to judge the urgency of the situation and to foresee possible dangers in time to act'.

These gaps in Paget's knowledge were at once to be filled, and on a generous scale. On the morning of the next day, Wednesday, March 18, he was closeted with the ministers and with French. What he then learnt and what orders were given him are so relevant to the course of subsequent events that they must be given in full.

Six possible situations with which he might have to deal on his return to take up his command were unfolded to him. There might be armed opposition to small bodies of troops moving to reinforce depots. There might be attacks on the depots or on the artillery at Dundalk. The blowing-up or destruction of railway lines might be attempted. Serious conflict might arise between Protestants and Roman Catholics in Belfast, following upon the proclamation of a Provisional Government, or arising out of the general excitement. He must not (and this brought his superiors to their fifth point) turn a blind eye on the chances of widespread sporadic disorder occurring in the south and west of Ireland and calling for the use of large numbers of troops to protect the scattered Protestants against the reprisals which might be made upon them by the Catholic population.

These were tall orders in themselves, but they were far from reaching the heights of responsibility to which Paget must climb. There was a sixth consideration he had to take into account — the possibility of 'an organized, war-like movement of Ulster Volunteers under their responsible leaders'. If that happened, it would have to be met by concentrated military force. If necessary, 'large reinforcements' would be sent to him from England.

But, he was reassured, the worst would very likely not come to the worst. No one in the Government believed that the precautionary troop movements he was being ordered to make would lead to bloodshed. Paget was not to be consoled either at that meeting or in the further discussions he had on the next day, Thursday, March 19, before he left by the night mail for Dublin. He tried desperately to get some concessions from Seely to his point of view and he succeeded, though, as he later said, 'only at a late hour' and then with the help of French. He went back with the assurance that officers actually domiciled in Ulster would be exempted from taking part in any operation that might take place. They would be permitted to 'disappear' — disappear was the word used at the War Office — and when all was over would be allowed to resume their places without their career or position being affected.

The briefing of Paget was not the only activity,

ministerial or unofficial, that filled these two busy days. It was agreed by Asquith on the Wednesday at a meeting at No. 10 Downing Street that troops should be moved to reinforce Omagh, Armagh, Dundalk, Enniskillen and Carrickfergus, that troops in Belfast should be moved out and that ships of the navy should be sent to make it a combined operation. The moves were to take place on Friday, March 20 and (as Major-General Friend on the spot was wired to by the reluctant Paget) 'to be complete by dawn, Saturday the 21st, with all secrecy'. So hurried was it all to be that Friend was ordered to move the battalion from the Victoria Barracks in Belfast 'with all ammunition and bolts of rifles, if unable to move rifles themselves'.

Macready was to go to Belfast with a dormant commission, to be used if and when he thought necessary, appointing him Military Governor in that city. After lunch on Wednesday, March 18, French, who had taken part in the discussions with Paget, sent for Wilson, who gathered that the Government contemplated scattering troops all over Ulster 'as though it were a Pontypool coal strike'. French had pointed out that this was opposed to all true strategy, but had been told that the political situation required that dispersion. French said that, as far as he could see, the Government was determined to see this thing through. Wilson thought the whole thing was a 'nightmare' and, before the day was out, was airing his views first to Amery and then, at dinner, to Milner, Jameson (of the raid) and Carson.

Carson, thus brought up to date with what was happening, knew what to say when the House met on Thursday, March 19. Bonar Law then moved a vote of censure, asking if Ulster were to be treated as 'a new Poland' and uttering the warning that if it were a question of civil war 'soldiers are citizens like the rest of us'. After Asquith had spoken, Carson rose. He reproached the

Prime Minister for having endorsed the provocation uttered by Churchill at Bradford. 'I feel I ought not to be here, but in Belfast.' A member interrupted, shouting 'With your sword drawn?' Carson then let himself go. Slapping the brass-bound boxes in front of him, he said, 'If this is the last word of the Government, what more have we to do here? Let the Government come and try conclusions with them in Ulster. Ulster is on the best of terms with the army. It is the only part of Ireland of which that can be said.' He asked them to think of the effect on the army of bringing it into armed conflict with the loyalists of Ulster. Pointing across the table at the ministers, he said, 'You will be sheltering yourselves behind the army. Under your directions they will become assassins. I hate all this talk about the army being sent to Ulster.'

There was no anger in his voice, but he quickly flared into anger when Devlin sneered at him as 'a young lawyer who deserted Home Rule and Liberalism when he saw a chance of bettering his fortunes'. 'The observation of the hon. member is an infamous lie, and he knows it', Carson rejoined. Instantly the House was in uproar. The Speaker expressed certainty that Carson would see that however strong his feelings, he had used an expression that was not to be used in the House of Commons. Carson withdrew 'infamous lie' and substituted 'wilful falsehood'. Having done so, he rose from the Front Opposition bench and proceeded to leave the chamber by the door behind the Speaker's chair. The Opposition rose to speed him on his way with prolonged and enthusiastic cheers. When he got to the side of the Speaker's chair, he looked down the chamber, raised his right arm and waved it. He had only left himself twenty minutes to catch his train at Euston for the Belfast boat. He did not miss it.

He and Paget arrived respectively at Belfast and at Dublin on the morning of Friday, March 20. But before

crossing with them, there is more to be said of the events
of Thursday, March 19. On that day Simon, whose legal
authority had been called in to help the Service ministers,
expressed to Seely some misgivings about the decision to
call Macready Military Governor in Belfast. 'My dear
Seely,' he wrote, 'I greatly deprecate [he underlined the
last two words] the expression "Military Governor".
Nothing could be more unfortunate, as it seems to me,
than to use the language of civil war when you are actually
making a special command to obviate civil war.' This
scruple was met, and it was made easier because Macready,
owing to illness, found himself unable to proceed immediately to Ireland. Friend was to be appointed as a temporary measure to take his place with the more innocuous
title of 'General Officer Commanding the Belfast District'.

It was on the afternoon of this Thursday that the
soldiers on the Curragh military camp, a few miles from
Dublin, received orders that all guards should be issued
with ball ammunition. An hour later this order was
widened; ammunition must be served out to every man
in barracks. These sudden orders startled the Curragh
garrison from top to bottom. They would have been even
more startled had they known of talks that were proceeding,
also on the afternoon of March 19, at the War Office.
There Wilson had an argument with the Director of
Military Training, Sir William Robertson. Wilson's
opponent had taken no part in all the political manœuvring.
His army career, which was to bring him to the rank of
Field-Marshal, had begun in the 'seventies when he had
taken the Queen's Shilling and enlisted in Gough's old
regiment, the 16th Lancers. A Lincolnshire village lad,
Robertson had won his commission from the ranks by
zeal for soldiering and rigid economy. He was already
being besieged by excited officers asking him what they
should do, and he had had no hesitation in telling them to
go away, make their minds easy and get on with their work,

as he felt sure that, in the long run, troops would not be
used against Ulster.

Now he learnt for the first time that he had been wrong,
and his first question on hearing what had been decided
brought him into conflict with Wilson. Which of them,
he wanted to know, would be responsible for making the
necessary arrangements and issuing the orders consequent
on the decision to reinforce Paget, if need arose for those
large 'reinforcements' from England. His voice comes as
the first sound of professional concern in how these
ambitious plans which were being made in the heat of the
moment were to be implemented. The responsibility for
operations *outside* the United Kingdom, Robertson pointed
out, rested with the Director of Military Operations
(Wilson); that for operations *inside*, but only as against
overseas attack, rested with the Director of Military
Training (Robertson), while the Adjutant-General (Ewart)
dealt with the use of troops in aid of the civil power.
Robertson, warming to his argument, explained that the
case of Ulster did not fall within any of these three spheres.
Each of the three generals protested that it was not his
business. But in the end Robertson lost; Wilson and
Ewart, to put it colloquially, 'passed the buck'. It was
decided that if troops had to be employed, the duty would
come under the heading of home defence and the arrangement would have to fall upon him. Resigned to his fate,
he was still determined to get to the bottom of what it was
all about. 'Are we supposed to be going to war with
Ulster, that is, will the troops be on "active service"? If
we are not going to war, what are we going to do, as the
case is obviously not one of supposed civil disorder because
there is no disorder at present? If we are going to war,
is mobilization to be ordered, and what ammunition,
supplies and transport are the troops to take?'

The answers to these pertinent questions were never
given; events moved too quickly to make it necessary to

dispose of them. But before they became academic, as they did within little more than twenty-four hours, the confusion prevailing at high Army levels had been communicated to the Navy. A spate of fleet orders were issued on Thursday, March 19, from the Admiralty. The vice-admiral commanding the 3rd battle squadron in Arosa Bay off Portugal received orders to sail at ordinary speed to Lamlash in the Firth of Clyde, opposite Belfast. After clearing Ushant, he was himself to proceed in his flag-ship to Plymouth, and come up to London, reporting at the Admiralty and subsequently rejoining his squadron at Lamlash, whither the flag-ship was to go direct. The senior naval officer at Bantry, in County Cork, was to send H.M.S. *Attentive* and H.M.S. *Pathfinder* to Kingstown, the port of Dublin, at sufficient speed to get there by noon on March 20. There the commanding officer of H.M.S. *Attentive* would be met by a staff officer from Dublin, and he was to embark one company of the Bedfordshire Regiment and to go on to Belfast Lough. Meanwhile, the captain of H.M.S. *Pathfinder* was personally to arrange with the senior military officer in Carrickfergus Castle for defending it against attack 'by every means'. If necessary, guns and searchlights from the ship were to be used. She was to arrive off Carrickfergus at daybreak on Saturday. The troops were to be landed at once. He himself would then land, in plain clothes, at Bangor in County Down and see Macready 'as to cooperation with the military in certain eventualities'.

The Commander-in-Chief of Portsmouth was to send a destroyer of the 4th flotilla to reach Kingstown next evening. Her task was to embark the General-Officer-Commanding-in-Chief Dublin, if necessary, and her commanding officer was to report himself to the general at the Royal Hospital, Dublin, and place himself at his orders. He was to wear plain clothes on shore. These three orders were scattered from Whitehall to Arosa Bay, Bantry and

Portsmouth between 1.57 P.M. and 2.32 P.M. on March 19. At 9 o'clock in the evening, the commanding officer of H.M.S. *Gibraltar* received orders to sail to Kingstown with H.M.S. *Royal Arthur* and to be prepared to embark next day 275 infantry in each ship for conveyance to Dundalk, where they were to be disembarked early on the following morning.

So ends the record of Thursday, March 19. A combined operation was under way. The Ulster Volunteers and any evil-disposed persons who might have it in mind to aid them were to find that the Royal Navy and the Army had taken over responsibility for preserving law and order in Ulster.

On Friday morning, March 20, Paget, back in Dublin, was able to wire to Seely that the transport of troops had been agreed by railway and that a battalion had left by train. This disposed of fears, telegraphically expressed by Friend on the previous day, that the Northern Railway might not agree to allow troop trains to travel. Paget also reported that all arrangements for the general situation had been made and that the commencement of all movements had started successfully.

Such satisfaction as this telegram gave to Seely was short-lived. It was followed, in the course of the day, by two further telegrams. The first carried the news that the commanding officer of the 5th Lancers reported that all his officers except two and one doubtful were resigning their commissions. Paget feared that the same conditions prevailed in the 16th Lancers. He further feared that the men would refuse to move. His second telegram was brief and more far-reaching. It ran 'Regret to report Brigadier and fifty-seven officers, 3rd Cavalry Brigade, prefer to accept dismissal if ordered north'. Mutiny, so it seemed to Seely and Churchill, had broken out at the Curragh.

K

CHAPTER X

THE CAVALRY WILL NOT RIDE

ON the evening of Thursday, March 19, Lady Alice Fergusson, the wife of Major-General Sir Charles Fergusson who commanded the 5th Division, wrote to Mrs. Gough, whose husband, Brigadier-General Gough, commanded the 3rd Cavalry Brigade, regretting that they could not dine that night, as her husband was so very busy giving orders for troop movements. Gough had been startled earlier in the day by the issue of ball ammunition mentioned in the last chapter. The inability of Fergusson to dine with him coming on top of this unusual issue 'woke him up' (the phrase is his own). He was busy at the time with cavalry squadron training and Allenby was inspecting his brigade. Allenby could throw no light on what was afoot, so Gough wrote a hurried letter to his brother, Johnnie, of the Rifle Brigade, now Chief Staff Officer to Haig at Aldershot. 'What the devil', Gough wrote, 'is up?'

The direct abruptness of this question was characteristic of the man who asked it. Upon him and Fergusson the burden of decision was now to fall. The politicians had played — had overplayed — their hand and it rested with these two soldiers to decide how the game would end. Both were Etonians who had passed through Sandhurst into famous regiments and proved their worth on active service. Gough was forty-three and Fergusson five years older. One was a Scot and the other Irish by blood and upbringing. They were, in spite of a certain community of background, as contrasted temperamentally as were Asquith and Carson.

Fergusson had succeeded, seven years before, to the ancient baronetcy of Kilkerran of which he was the seventh holder. Gazetted to the Grenadier Guards before his eighteenth birthday, he had been attached to the Egyptian Army and greatly distinguished himself in Kitchener's campaign in the Sudan. After a spell as Adjutant-General of the Egyptian Army, he had commanded the 3rd battalion of his regiment, from which he was promoted to the newly created appointment of Inspector of Infantry. He had succeeded to command of the 5th Division in 1913 and so was one of the most senior officers to be confronted by Paget. Fergusson's later career in the 1914–18 war and then as Governor-General and Commander-in-Chief of New Zealand confirmed the early promise of an officer cool in dangerous circumstances and not easily provoked.

Gough's prowess in action had already been displayed and was to be again. At twenty-four he was the youngest captain in the Army ; he became the youngest commanding officer, youngest general and, finally, the youngest Army commander in the First World War. His father and one of his uncles were V.C.'s. An earlier ancestor had led the 87th to an attack in the Peninsular War, calling out in Irish 'Faugh-a-Ballagh' (Clear the way) to his men — a battle-cry subsequently adopted as their motto by the Royal Irish Fusiliers and by the Gough family.

He had been at Eton with the son of Roberts who won the V.C. in the South African War, and he had served under the veteran Field-Marshal. As a Scarlet Lancer, he had seen and disapproved of Churchill on the Indian frontier. Churchill, whom he recalled as a 'fresh-faced, fair-haired subaltern of the 4th Hussars', had 'talked a great deal'. They met at a mess in Peshawar and Gough noted how Churchill 'used to take up his stand in front of the fire and from that position of advantage lecture all and sundry with complete confidence — it seemed to me that he was practising making speeches. . . . Brought up in the 16th

Lancers, I did not at all approve of this somewhat bumptious attitude. Such style would never have been tolerated in our mess, but in the Gunners' Mess at Peshawar neither the many generals who gathered there nor anyone else attempted·to check him. I used to wonder how the generals stood it, but even then I was dimly aware that they were rather afraid of him and his pen.'

Gough was afraid of no one's pen or tongue. He had been the first officer of Buller's relieving force to enter Ladysmith and he had got there by a Nelsonian disregard for authority. 'I had just reached the ridge in front of me', he has related, 'when an orderly galloped up and thrust a note into my hand. It was an order from Dundonald "to retire at once". This last shell fired by the Boers shook him, and it might have succeeded in bringing our entry into Ladysmith that day to an abrupt conclusion! . . . I had not the slightest intention of obeying the order to retire. I just crumpled the note up and threw it to the ground, telling the orderly to return to Dundonald and report that he had delivered the message.'

Fergusson would have agreed with Gough's affirmation of faith, 'I am a firm supporter of the old school tie', but they wore it with a difference. Together, these two officers with several others caught the early morning train from the Curragh to Dublin. There, half an hour later, Paget came into the Conference room. He was smoking a cigar and his head was still reeling from the fumes of those London talks. There were present, besides Fergusson and Gough, Major-General Friend, the Director of Administration, three infantry brigadier generals and the colonel commanding the 11th district. Paget's personal staff officers did not attend.

Both Fergusson and Paget set down, immediately after this Conference, what was said. According to Fergusson, the Commander of the Forces began by saying that what he had to say might appear theatrical. But the situation was very serious. Certain measures were to be taken, and it was conceivable that trouble would result. The whole place would be in a blaze, he thought, tomorrow. Precautionary measures had already been taken, and he detailed those which had already taken place. There were warships at Belfast Lough, at Kingstown and at Lamlash. Other troops would in the event of disturbance have to be moved. 'I think he added [at this Conference] that in the event of such disturbance, such an enormous force would be displayed that Ulster would be convinced of the impossibility of resistance. I am not clear whether it was on this occasion, or in the afternoon, that he explained the reason. This was, that the Government were determined that no aggressive act on their part should start the conflict. If anyone started the fighting, it should be the Ulstermen. Should they anticipate the Government by occupying those buildings the Government would be forced to turn them out, and bloodshed would result. By occupying those buildings now, the onus of any aggressive act would fall on the Ulstermen. He reiterated over and over again that there was to be no aggression on the part of the troops; he would expect them to accept punishment without returning the fire, in the hopes that an opportunity would offer for parley, and the Government terms accepted.

'Sir Arthur Paget then said that he had been in close consultation at the War Office until a late hour the previous evening. He said that the promise that had been made him some time ago, to the effect that opportunity would be given in good time to Officers who wished to resign to do so, could not be kept, as the situation had arisen suddenly. He had after much persuasion been able only to secure from the War Minister certain concessions. He had first succeeded in persuading Sir John French, had told him that he could make no impression on the Minister for War, and subsequently at the last moment by Sir John's help had obtained the following concessions from Colonel Seely.

'*First* : Officers actually domiciled in Ulster would be exempted from taking part in any operations that might take place. They would be permitted to 'disappear' (that being the exact phrase used by the War Office), and when all was over would be allowed to resume their places without their career or position being affected.

'*Second* : Officers who stated they were unwilling to serve might tender their resignations, but these could not be accepted. And Officers doing so would be forthwith dismissed from the Service.'

[In the afternoon, I think, Sir Arthur added that they would probably be tried by Court Martial, or, if not, dismissed without that formality.]

'The phrase "domiciled in Ulster" was to be strictly interpreted as those who actually had their homes within that province. They must certify this on paper, and must give their word of honour to take no part in any operations on the side of Ulster. Brigadiers were to be held responsible, under penalty of Court Martial, that they had verified as far as possible the genuineness of such applications.

'Sir Arthur referred to the difficulty of obtaining these concessions, and said that the War Minister had, with regard to the latter class, said "I hope there will be very few of these".

'Sir Arthur then said that if any of us present was not prepared to take his part he must come to a decision, and in that case he must not attend the second conference to be held that afternoon, as none but those who were prepared to do their duty could be admitted to further councils. Brigadiers were to go at once and put the alternatives before their officers. Decisions must be prompt, and the numbers who were not prepared to do their duty notified without delay, if possible by that evening. Turning to

General Gough, he said that a squadron of Cavalry from Dublin was to be held in readiness to march northwards next morning if required.

'He then said, "Has anyone any remarks to make?" The only one who spoke; after a pause, was General Gough, who pointed out that although his home was not actually in Ulster, he was intimately associated with that part of Ireland. Sir Arthur replied that the domicile condition was absolutely to be strictly interpreted, and that he [General Gough] could not be held to come under that Clause.

'The officers present then withdrew. Sir Arthur's last remark was "Tell your Officers to trust me, and I will guarantee that there shall be no bloodshed".'

Gough's account, also written at the time, adds some colour. Paget, he records, warned him that he need expect 'no mercy' from his old friend at the War Office, meaning, presumably, French. The only effect of this menace on Gough was 'to put up my hackles at once. Why should I be picked out to be threatened?' Paget told them, according to Gough, that he would explain at another meeting at two o'clock in the afternoon, which was not to be attended by any officers who were 'not prepared to carry out everything that he then ordered'. As Gough left the room, Paget 'addressed a remark to me personally, why I cannot think, "You need not expect any help from the other side"'.

'Directly we left the room,' Gough continues, 'Fergusson said "Come along and let us talk over this." Rolt [one of the Infantry Brigade generals] came with us. Fergusson was very agitated, white and cheeks trembling. As soon as we got outside he began arguing "that the army must hold together, that we must not break up the army, etc." Rolt seemed very averse to going against Ulster. I did not argue. I listened. Fergusson went away saying that he had decided to go. I said I would not go.'

The record of the morning may now be carried on by Fergusson. He states that his brigadiers went off to their commands, to interview the officers. He drew up a memorandum for the unit commanders of the division, who had not been present at the Conference, embodying the terms that were to be put to them and their officers and dispatched it by his A.D.C., who was sent off by train to the Curragh.

Meanwhile, Gough drove off by motor to Kingsbridge where one of his regiments, the 5th Lancers, was stationed. On arrival he telegraphed to his brother at Aldershot, telling him of the alternatives put by Paget, and of his own decision. Colonel Parker of the 5th Lancers, on hearing what had happened, threw himself on his sofa — they were in his study — and said, 'It is monstrous, monstrous, I won't go, I won't go'. They went back to the officers' mess and told all the officers they could collect — about fifteen — of the alternatives. Gough said that these were big crises and that every man must decide for himself according to his conscience.

He then left the barracks and went straight back to Headquarters, where he saw Friend. He told him of his decision. Friend was very nice and seemed very sorry. He asked Gough 'if I could look upon it as he did, merely to maintain law and order. I said — No, if it was law and order now, it might develop into civil war at any moment and then it would be much worse and dishonourable to leave Paget, and therefore it was better and more honourable to do it at once.' Friend then asked if Gough would see Paget. 'I said I would rather not, as it could not alter my decision and would only be painful to us both, but I asked him to convey to Paget that my decision was not caused by any feelings towards himself and that I thought he had done his best for us in the matter of terms at the War Office.

'I then asked Friend what he wanted me to do, and said

MAJOR-GENERAL SIR CHARLES FERGUSSON

that I looked upon myself as dismissed the Service and expected to see myself in the *Gazette* as such on Tuesday. Friend said that I had better carry on as usual for the present and send my letter that evening asking to "retire". But he said that he would speak to Paget first and warn him (which he did at 4.20 P.M.). I then asked him what action he required of me as regards the units in my Brigade? Friend said that I was to see the officers and find out the numbers of those who were prepared to accept dismissal and that the results were to be wired to him that evening. I told him that I had seen the 5th Lancers already, and that though I knew nothing definite and no figures, I thought at least twenty would not go and would rather be dismissed. He seemed surprised, and upset, and begged me to let him know the results soon, as "if there were many resignations it might make the Government alter their policy". I then left.'

So ended a busy morning. At 2 o'clock in the afternoon the second Conference was held at the Royal Hospital. There were present Major-General Pulteney and two of his brigade generals of the 4th Division, Fergusson, Friend and two officers of the Headquarters staff. Friend reported that Gough had declined to attend, and Paget expressed great regret at this decision. The proceedings of this Conference were described in writing at the time by Fergusson as follows:

'Sir Arthur then went into details already given at the first Conference. He and the Staff Officers present supplemented them by further explanations, giving in detail the force that was to be used in Ireland.

'I understood that should there be any disturbance in the north, the 5th Division supplemented by the 11th Brigade from Colchester would move probably to the line of the Boyne. It would be reinforced by the 1st Division from Aldershot. The 6th Division, less necessary garrisons for the south which were subsequently worked out by

Generals Pulteney and Friend, would move to Dublin
reinforced by the 18th Infantry Brigade from England.
The 3 Infantry Battalions from Scotland and some Artillery
would land in the north, and I understood would garrison
certain points forming a ring round Belfast, *i.e.* Larne —
Ballymena — some point west of Belfast — Lisburn —
Holywood — Bangor, which latter was to be the naval base.
A Naval Brigade was to be landed at Bangor.

'It was explained at length that there was to be no
act of aggression — that a big demonstration would, it was
hoped, meet the case. No firing on any consideration
until Sir Arthur personally authorized it, and that order
would not be given until [as explained in the morning] all
other means had failed. Meanwhile, strict orders were to
be given to all detachments that on no account must there
be any conflict with the opposing side. If a party of troops
out of Barracks were molested or their progress impeded,
they were to withdraw to Barracks.

'At 2.45 P.M. the 6th Division Brigadiers left to return
to their commands, and shortly afterwards the Conference
broke up. I returned to the Curragh by the 4.15 train.

'The impression left on my mind by the events of the
day were genuinely that the measures to be taken were
primarily precautionary. The occupation of the Government Buildings in Belfast did not seem to be in any way
intended as a provocative measure; the reason explained
to us seemed perfectly natural and reasonable. It was
conceivable, however, that some of the Ulster adherents
might get out of hand and attack the police, and thus
initiate an outbreak, which would entail the adoption of
the preliminary measures already decided on and further
movements of troops in support. The reasons given by
Sir Arthur Paget for the reinforcements from England as
a demonstration also seemed comprehensible. It never
occurred to me from anything that was said that any
provocative act was contemplated, or that there would be

any further movement at all unless disturbances ensued on the occupation of the Government Buildings.

'Sir Arthur Paget said more than once: "They wanted to use the soldiers as a bait [*i.e.* in occupying the Government Buildings in Belfast], but I would not have that, and told them it was a matter for the Civil Power, not for soldiers".

'This expression, however, conveyed nothing to me beyond that the occupation of the Buildings was considered a necessity, and yet might possibly lead to disturbance; and hence the necessity of being prepared for all eventualities.

'During the conversations [I do not remember when] I said to Sir Arthur Paget that presumably the order was from the King. He replied, "Do you think for a moment that I would accept it unless I knew it had the sanction of the King? Of course it is his order." He was so emphatic that I had no hesitation afterwards in repeating this, when I considered it necessary, to Officers and men. And I reported that evening [Friday] that I had done so.

'He further said that it was reported by the Secret Service that great internal trouble was brewing in London, Liverpool and other large towns, and that there was great anxiety on this score. I understood him to say that the Labour Party was determined to make a big effort to advance their policy by taking advantage of the crisis. Anyhow the impression left on my mind was that an internal convulsion of the country was a probability of the near future.

'I do not think there is anything further to note with reference to these conferences except that officers were to be recalled from leave, and that troops might be called on to move at short notice.'

The scene then shifted to the Curragh, where Gough had gone by train immediately after lunch and Fergusson followed as soon as Paget's second Conference had ended. It was not the first time in its history that this wide plain in County Kildare, some thirty miles south-west of Dublin, had staged an exciting drama. 'Curragh' means a race-course, and chariot races are said to have taken place there as early as the first century A.D. But racing was not the only activity that it had seen. As a convenient meeting-place for the southern Irish, the Curragh had been the battle-ground of the kings of Meath, Leinster and Offaly. A Viceroy had there defeated a medieval Earl of Pembroke and, rather more than a century later, a Prior of Connell, leading an Irish force, had been routed by the English. The United Irishmen had gathered at the Curragh to the number of 30,000 during the Napoleonic wars. A British military camp had been established at the time of the Crimean War. And there, when not disturbed by politics, the cavalry and all arms of the Service trained.

There was no training on March 20, or, if there was, it did not go on under the eyes of commanding officers. Gough, on getting to the Curragh, explained the situation to the officers of his old regiment, the 16th Lancers. Having done so, he retired to his office with several of the seniors to talk matters over. It was at this discussion that Major Howell, of the 4th Hussars, suggested that it would be prudent to play for time. Major Howell had only recently joined the 4th Hussars from the Indian Cavalry. He was a calm, humorous man, and accustomed to expressing himself on paper. He had more than once acted as a special correspondent in India and in the Balkans for *The Times*.

At his instigation, a minute was prepared for Gough to have dispatched as quickly as possible to the Headquarters of the Irish Command. This minute was later to be praised by Asquith and Churchill, and to be printed in the White Paper they reluctantly published. It ran:

'With reference to the communication from the War Office conveyed to me verbally by the Commander-in-Chief this morning, I have the honour to report the result of my interviews with the officers of my brigade.

'The officers are of unanimous opinion that further
information is essential before they are called upon at such
short notice to take decisions so vitally affecting their
whole future, and especially that a clear definition should
be given of the terms "Duty as ordered" and "active
operations" in Ulster.

'If such duty consists of the maintenance of order and
the preservation of property, all the officers of this brigade,
including myself, would be prepared to carry out that duty.

'But if the duty involves the *initiation* of active military operations against Ulster, the following numbers of
officers by regiments would respectfully, and under protest,
prefer to be dismissed :

> Brigade Staff, 2 officers.
> 4th Hussars, 17 out of 19 doing duty.
> 5th Lancers, 17 out of 20 doing duty.
> 16th Lancers, 16 out of 16 doing duty.
> 3rd Brigade, Royal Horse Artillery, 6 out of 13 doing
>   duty, "including R.M."
> 4th Field Troop, Royal Engineers, 1 out of 1 doing
>   duty.
> 3rd Signal Troop, Royal Engineers, 1 out of 1 doing
>   duty.

In addition, the following are domiciled in Ulster and claim
protection as such :

> 4th Hussars, 2 officers.
> 5th Lancers, 1 officer.
> 3rd Brigade, Royal Horse Artillery, 2 officers.'

Fergusson followed Gough to the Curragh, getting
there at about 5.45. He met all the staff officers of the
Royal Engineers and Army Service Corps and he asked
for their decisions. They all said they detested the use of
troops against Ulster, resented the way in which their
decisions had been demanded at short notice and finally

declared that they would, under protest, do their duty as
ordered. They told Fergusson that, with a few exceptions,
their officers were prepared to follow them. This was
encouraging to Fergusson, but bad news immediately
followed. He learnt of the decision of the 3rd Cavalry
Brigade and undertook to forward Gough's minute to
Headquarters by the A.D.C., who left for Dublin at 8 P.M.,
also taking Fergusson's report to Paget. The cavalry
leaders tried to persuade Fergusson to write on similar
lines to the Gough minute, but he declined.

Paget, as was shown in the last chapter, had kept the
War Office in touch with the actions of the cavalry. The
reactions from London were prompt and emphatic.
Paget's second telegram reporting the preference of Gough
and his officers for dismissal if ordered north was answered
within less than half an hour. The War Office received it
at 11.35 P.M. At midnight a telegram from Seely was
dispatched. It read:

'Your telegram with reference to 5th and 16th Lancers
received. You have authority of Army Council to suspend
from duty any senior officers who have tendered their resignations or in any other manner disputed your authority.

'Take whatever action you think proper and report to
the War Office.

'Direct Gough and Officers Commanding 5th and 16th
Lancers to report themselves to the Adjutant-General at
the War Office without delay. They should leave by first
possible boat. They should be relieved of their Commands,
and officers are being sent to relieve them at once.

'Resignations of all officers should be refused.'

Armed with this drastic directive, Paget sped down to
the Curragh on Saturday morning to have it out with the
cavalrymen. The morning papers had carried stories that
trouble was afoot, and the camp had been invaded by
journalists. While Paget was closeted with Gough and his
officers, Mrs. Howell watched the journalists driving up

in side-cars, 'wandering about like pelicans in the wilderness and seeking vainly for any information, the ordinary Tommy not having the least idea what it was all about, and apparently taking little interest. Wives of officers in the brigade were in tears in the main Curragh street.'

Some thirty-five officers attended the meeting in barracks, including the colonels of the 4th Hussars, 16th Lancers and of the Royal Horse Artillery. This is Gough's contemporary note of the proceedings:

'At 11 A.M. Sir A. Paget entered the room and sat at the only table, asking us to sit down, which we did as best we could on the available accommodation.

'Sir A. Paget commenced by saying that he was our friend and asked us to trust him as our General and our Chief and he would see that we were not placed in any positions which we might object to. He said he did not know why so many officers had resigned because he had no intention of making war on Ulster, and to prove it he would take us into his confidence and divulge some of his "plans". Only units had been ordered that were necessary to protect "stores", etc., and even these moves were precautions mainly directed against the "Hibernians". The "depot" at Enniskillen was dangerously exposed to Hibernians; "his" guns in Dundalk — a low-lying town surrounded by hills "peopled" by Hibernians — were very exposed and every soldier would know that guns must have the protection of other arms.

'He had moved some troops by sea (he now thought it was a mistake) — merely to avoid their marching through the streets of Belfast — why should we think that military operations were intended against Ulster when everywhere his troops have been received with ovation in Ulster? To such an extent was he prepared to go to avoid fighting that he had given orders that if any Battalion met with opposition in its march it was to turn round and go back to barracks.

'And if fighting took place against Ulster Forces he

would order all his men to lie down and not return the fire and then "he and his Generals" would advance alone through the firing line and parley with the men of Ulster.

'As far as the Cavalry were concerned they would not be required to take any serious part in the fighting — not more than one regiment would be employed anyhow — and he would send one regiment south to maintain order there. A squadron or two might be employed on the lines of communication.

'Of course he would have to employ some scouts for "of course he did not want to march along and bump unexpectedly into a large force of the enemy". (Note — but no war was contemplated.) These scouts need not fire a shot, they would only bring him information, "just as they do at manœuvres". Even if a squadron should be on his flank in an engagement, "of course, if it cleared his flank for him he would be very pleased", but if it took no active part he would be content.

'He then went on to say that it was necessary of course "to hold the line of the Boyne" while 25,000 troops were being brought over from England. (Note — he said there was to be no war previously.)

'He said that he had expected that only a "few religious fanatics" would accept dismissal.

'He said that if officers liked to "indulge in the luxury of sentiment" they must pay for it, like other things. He said that no resignations would be accepted. He said that senior officers would be tried by Court-martial. He said that we must clearly understand that this was the direct order of "the Sovereign" and asked us "if we thought he would obey the orders of those dirty swine of politicians".

'Then, as no move took place, he said we must decide again and let General Fergusson know, and that if there was no change, that I and the C.O.'s would "hand over command", cross to London that night and report to the War Office next morning.

SIR ARTHUR PAGET

BRIGADIER-GENERAL
SIR HUBERT GOUGH

'Some of these statements were made in the presence only of myself, Major Kearsley, Cols. Breeks, MacEwen and Hogg.

'Colonel Breeks had some heated words with Sir A. Paget, but I have forgotten exactly what they were; they were mainly expressing the resentment felt at the grave decision demanded from officers, apparently for no cause, in a very short time and with practically a pistol at one's head.

'I remarked that I did not see how resignations could be refused, as they had been demanded from officers by the Chief's own orders. Also that though sentiment might be a luxury, men had died for it. Sir A. Paget also remarked that I need expect "no mercy" from Sir J. French and I replied that I did not ask any mercy.

'Sir A. Paget then left.

'Officers considered his speech. The majority seemed to think it unsatisfactory, both from the point of view of assurances offered that no organized attack was intended on Ulster, and also from the puerile and dishonest suggestions and subterfuges put forward.'

The meeting was evidently confused and stormy. Other officers who were present made notes at the time of what they recollected. One of them recorded that Paget stated that:

'1. In case of a collision with the Ulster army, he would reverse the ordinary procedure and go forward in front of the firing line with his staff. After the first burst of firing, he would hoist the white flag and confer with the Ulster Volunteers leaders and then go home.

'2. The cavalry need not fight but could run away or hoist the white flag if it came to the pinch.

'3. In the event of a big battle, the cavalry would be placed out of the way on the flank and need not take part — though if he were getting the worst of it, it would be up to the cavalry to help him.

L

'4. Disgrace was being brought on famous generals by the action of officers.

'5. It was not a soldier's job to indulge in sickly sentiment.

'6. He would march infantry to the cavalry lines and disarm the regiments concerned.

'7. The Ulstermen would be forced to fire the first shot.

'8. He would never have agreed to these operations if he did not know it was the King's wish.

'9. If officers refused to come in, there were worse things than dismissal, as they would find out.

'10. There was not an inch between the two parties in Parliament, so near were we to a settlement of the whole question.

'11. It was not worth while sacrificing our careers when the whole thing might be over next day.

'12. Ulster seemed quiet, but the government had made one dangerous move which he was not at liberty to disclose but which might cause an immediate rising in Ulster.'

The general impression left by Paget's appeal was summed up by another officer in these words: 'His idea of a sort of pantomime battle revolted us.'

While Paget was thus failing to shake the resolution of the cavalry, Fergusson was spending a more fruitful Saturday. He described it as follows:

'On reaching my office about 9 A.M. I met Brigadier Generals Rolt and Headlam, Commanding 14th Infantry Brigade and Artillery. They told me that the situation was very serious. The example of the 3rd Cavalry Brigade had become known, and many Officers, in some units practically all, were prepared to resign. At 9.30 I saw the 21 Suffolk Regiment in the Gymnasium. First I saw the Officers privately. Their attitude was very strained, in some cases almost truculent. After speaking to them I addressed the battalion as a whole. Half an hour later I saw the Officers and men of the 2nd Bn. Manchester Regiment in the same way. They were more amenable in their manner than the first-named Battalion, but obviously the feeling was very strong.

'I then motored to Kildare and afterwards to Newbridge, addressing Officers and men of the Artillery in the same way. Here the atmosphere was rather different, in the sense that there seemed less resentment, though many senior Officers were obviously torn in two as to what it was their duty to do. Some of the scenes were very painful. Before leaving both these places, however, I was assured of their support in the line I advocated. At Newbridge the example of the R. Horse Artillery had obviously had its effect in upsetting the situation.

'I did not use exactly the same arguments to all units, though generally my remarks were similar. In some cases it seemed necessary to say more than in others; in some cases questions were put showing the special difficulties which presented themselves to the minds of Officers.

'I told them that the first duty of soldiers was to obey the orders of their King and of constituted authority. I said this order was the King's and must have been issued with his sanction. That, for me, was enough.

'I pointed out the responsibility of influencing those under us. Personal considerations must give way to the duties of our respective positions as commanders of troops. I would be no party to any thing that tended to weaken discipline. Logically, we Officers could not refuse to obey the present orders, and yet expect our men to obey orders when they, on strike duty for instance, were placed in difficulties similar to those now confronting us.

'I spoke of the far reaching consequences of a disruption of the Army. That the country without a disciplined and united Army would be at the mercy of the mob. I alluded to the probability of even bigger questions arising if the Army broke up, that the Monarchy, Society and the Empire itself might be shattered.

'Finally I assured all that no aggressive measures of any kind were contemplated or would be tolerated; and in cases where further assurances on the point seemed necessary, I quoted the statements of the Commander of the Forces to that effect.

'I admit that I used the King's name freely; it was the most effective argument with those who were most stubborn. Loyalty to the King was in fact the determining factor in inducing many Officers to withhold their resignations.

'The Commander of the Forces interviewed the Officers of the Cavalry Brigade about noon, and left it to me to receive their decisions, and if these were adverse to issue certain orders to their senior Officers. I tried hard to influence General Gough and his Commanding Officers, but without success.

'In the afternoon I went to Dublin and interviewed the officers of the 11 East Surrey Regiment and all Officers of the 13th Infantry Brigade who were "doubtful". This interview was also successful.

'I reported the situation to the Commander of the Forces at the Royal Hospital about 7.30 P.M., and returned to the Curragh.'

On Saturday night, Gough and the Colonels crossed to England in obedience to Seely's telegram.

CHAPTER XI

OFF TO LONDON

LONDON had begun to buzz with rumours as early as Friday night. Austen Chamberlain, dining with the Salisburys, was told on arrival by Lady Helen Cassel, 'You know that the fleet is ordered to Belfast and that Sir Arthur Paget is to be reinforced with 60,000 troops'. Chamberlain expressed his doubts. The lady stuck to her point. 'But it is!' she said. 'Miss Paget overheard her brother saying so. She at once told Almeric and he told Felix.' After dinner the butler told Chamberlain that General Gough was waiting in the hall to see him. He went out and found the General (the brother of the cavalry commander) greatly excited, and having with him the telegram from Ireland.

At 9.30 next morning Wilson was round at Bonar Law's, telling him 'how serious everything was and how, on my present information, I thought it would be imperative to back Hubert'. This was the beginning of a busy day for Wilson. He had interviews with French and Seely. He drafted a promise to be made by the Government to reinstate all officers. French took this draft to Seely, but gathered that 'it was not agreeable to Asquith and his crowd'. At a quarter to eight in the evening Bonar Law came to see Wilson and 'we talked over the events of the day'. Wilson was half inclined to follow Gough's lead. 'I am more than ever determined to resign, but I cannot think of a really good way of doing it.'

The day had been a most harassing one for the King. The first he knew of what had happened was when he opened his newspaper. He cancelled part of his projected visit to Lancashire, saw Seely and, as he noted in the royal diary, spoke very strongly to him. Roberts came to see him 'and was in despair about it all and said it would ruin the army'. An interview with French followed, in which the King impressed upon the General that 'if great tact were not shown, there would be no army left'. Having written a well-justified letter of complaint to Asquith — his indignation being the stronger because he gathered that his own name had been too freely used — he ended the day with the entry, 'We dined alone, read in the evening. Bed at 11, very tired.' It would be interesting to know what the King said at dinner about the politicians and the generals.

Asquith too was kept busy. He heard for the first time on Saturday morning that the Admiralty had ordered the movement of a battle squadron. Ambitious plans for throwing in — should occasion arise — the strength of the Navy were promptly wrecked by him as thoroughly as the winds and the Elizabethan sailors dispersed the Armada.

Unfortunately for the Government, two of its pillars remained unaware on Saturday of how ill the Ulster adventure had prospered. Lloyd George was away in Huddersfield and, believing that all was going well, he delivered a speech as pugnacious as Churchill's recent one at Bradford. He called Ulster a spoilt child and he breathed defiance. 'I am here this afternoon on behalf of the British Government,' he declared, 'to say this to you — that they mean to confront this defiance of popular liberties with a most resolute unwavering determination whatever the hazard may be.' *The Times* described this as 'the speech of an incendiary, eager to pour oil upon the flames'.

Poor Spender also put his foot into it. He was generally kept in closest touch with what was happening in the inner circles of the Cabinet, but on this occasion his information had been overtaken by events. On Saturday his paper, the *Westminster Gazette*, contained a complacent leading article. The Government, it ran, 'is bound to have on the spot such a force as will secure the country against riot and prevent any group of men taking the law into their own hands and precipitating a conflict which might lead to determined fighting. When that is done, we shall be able to resume the politics of the Irish question as politics and not as threats in a process of civil tumult. From that moment the prospect of settlement will, we believe, improve.' When that leader was read in the London clubs, there was loud laughter, for it was already known to a widening circle that the Government, so far from having got the upper hand, was seeking desperately for a way of escape from the dilemma into which the cavalry officers had plunged it.

Gough on Sunday morning went to his mother's flat in Sloane Square. His brother from Aldershot joined him at 9 o'clock with the encouraging news that the line the War Office meant to take was that there had been a complete misunderstanding, that the alternatives put before him by Paget should never have been put, and that they were to be reinstated. But this did not leave Gough in a melting mood. He was both thoroughly roused and deeply suspicious of his superiors, civil and military, and he had made up his mind that the only honourable course open to him was to leave the Service. They went over to the War Office at 9.45 A.M., meeting Colonel MacEwen of the 16th Lancers in the street and finding Colonel Parker of the 5th Lancers sitting in the hall by the fire. Gough made rough notes of the scene.

'All cheery, quite firm as to our attitude, and quite indifferent as to whether we returned to our positions and the army or not; we were certainly not prepared to do so, if we were liable to be exposed again to such a situation as had been forced upon us by Paget, nor under any conditions were we prepared to undertake war on Ulster.

'At about 10.15 A.M. shown into Ewart's waiting room. I was put in a separate room to Colonels MacEwen and Parker. Shortly after I was shown into Ewart's room. Found him and another. My manner expressed my feelings, I was very stiff. I was determined that under no circumstances would I submit to any form of lecture or "wigging". I was fully conscious of having committed no offence, and equally conscious that a most cruel and hard position had been forced upon me and other officers by the War Office and Paget —, which filled me and the other officers with resentment. General Ewart came forward very nicely and introduced me to General Macready. General Ewart asked me to sit down, and said this was a very grave business. I replied very sharply "I am fully aware of that".

General Ewart said he merely wanted to get from me the facts of what had occurred.

'General Macready began taking pencil notes. I immediately demanded that I should be given a copy of everything that was written down. I never got this copy, as I did not think that anything very material had been said of which I had not already got a copy.

'General Ewart asked me if I thought any officer had any right to question when he should go, or should not go, in support of the Civil Power to maintain law and order. I said "None whatever" and I added if Sir A. P. had "ordered" my Brigade to Belfast we would have gone without demur, although I could not think why we should be wanted there.

'The interview then closed, and I was ordered to remain in London within hail of the telephone.

'Colonels MacEwen and Parker then went in and gave their evidence.

'While we were in the War Office we met Colonel Hill who had been giving his evidence. This was the first intimation we had received that Colonel Hill had also resigned on Friday morning; he told me that he also had stated that on Friday Sir A. P. had told us that "he expected the country would be in a blaze by Saturday".

'Later on in the afternoon I received order to attend W.O. at 11 A.M. next day.'

That Sunday evening Asquith gave a statement to *The Times* for publication on Monday. It was a masterpiece of understatement. The recent movements of troops were, it declared, purely precautionary and intended only to safeguard depots of arms. 'As for the so-called naval movements, they simply consisted in the use of two small cruisers to convey a detachment of troops to Carrickfergus without the necessity of marching them through the streets of Belfast. No further movements of troops are in contemplation.' No warrants had been issued for the arrest of the Ulster leaders and no such step was contemplated.

Asquith dealt finally with what he described as 'the third misapprehension'. It concerned officers at the Curragh. There was to be no general inquisition into the intentions of these officers in the event of their being asked to take up arms against Ulster. 'No such action is intended, if only for the reason that the employment of troops against Ulster is a contingency which the Government hopes may never arise.'

Much was to be heard in the days ahead of this statement, especially as to the reference to the fleet, and Asquith, in due course, and as will be seen, explained in Parliament why he was so economical in his handling of the full facts. His preoccupation on the Sunday night and Monday morning was to ensure that Gough and his subordinates returned to their duties and that the normal routine of the army should not be upset. It was by now plain that Paget had addressed the officers in terms that could not be defended and that gave the cavalry an honourable case for protesting that they had not refused to obey a formal

order. On the contrary, they had been offered highly
muddling alternatives. Further, it was clear that a settlement must be reached before the House of Commons had
to be met on Monday.

So the morning was a hectic one. Haig came up from
Aldershot and saw Gough. At 11.15 Gough saw French
and Ewart. French began by saying that he was Gough's
'old friend and chief' and wished to be trusted and to be
believed when he said that there had been 'a great misunderstanding'. Gough records that 'Sir John was very
suave in his manner, I very stiff. . . . I at once said
"There has been *NO* misunderstanding on *my* part, Sir".'
French continued, 'As there had been misunderstanding
you are all to return to your commands as if nothing had
happened'. Gough said, 'I am quite willing to do that,
but such a grave crisis has arisen that neither I nor the
officers can return unless we receive a definite assurance
that we shall not be asked again to enforce on Ulster the
present Home Rule Bill'. French at once said that he
could give such an assurance. Gough demanded it in
writing. French appealed to him : 'Is my word not good
enough ?' adding, 'Let's wipe everything off the slate and
go back to Thursday evening'. Gough stood out for a
written assurance. French said it was impossible. Gough
refused to return without it. French threw himself into a
chair. A long and painful silence ensued. Gough kept
his eye on the toe of his boot. French said, 'Very well,
there is nothing for it but to take him before the Secretary
of State'.

The three officers went down the passage to Seely's
room. On the way, French took Gough's arm and said,
'For God's sake, go back and don't make any more
difficulties, you don't know how serious all this is. If you
don't go back, all the War Office will resign. I have done
my best for you. If they had attempted to penalise you,
I would have resigned myself.' Gough said he was

'awfully grateful'. The three Generals entered Seely's room and found Paget there. Seely's manner, so Gough recalls, 'expressed extreme hauteur. He was most stiff to French and Ewart and honoured me with a glare! He very haughtily pointed to various chairs and directed us to be seated in those he patted. I was very struck with the submissive attitude of French, Paget and Ewart.

'As soon as we were seated Colonel Seely in a very truculent manner turned his eyes on me and attempted to browbeat me and to stare me out of countenance.

'I was not going to allow this, and he eventually dropped his eyes. His manner then altered. From excessive truculence, he went to that of superior wisdom.

'He commenced a long discourse, explaining to me the relation of the military to the civil power, that in order to maintain law and order the civil power was justified in using the force necessary, but no more — etc. etc. I knew all this very well, as it was taken almost verbatim from the Manual of Military Law. I listened with attention, however, in order to discover if possible what point he was endeavouring to make, and to be on my guard in case he attempted to place me in a disadvantageous position.'

There followed an argument, Gough insisting on a written assurance, and Seely maintaining that it was impossible. French then intervened to say that 'perhaps General Gough has not made it quite clear that he feels that he will not be able to reassure his officers or regain their confidence unless he can show them the authority of the Army Council; and that he feels that his own verbal assurance will not be sufficient now that feeling has been so greatly aroused'. Seely clutched at this straw; turning to Paget, he said, 'I see, I think that is only a reasonable request'. Ewart was asked to draw up a draft.

Its fate must now be followed into the Cabinet, whither it was taken. What precisely happened is not clear, because the principal actors have left somewhat conflicting accounts, but several material points are established beyond dispute. First, the Cabinet approved three paragraphs. They read:

'You are authorized by the Army Council to inform the Officers of the 3rd Cavalry Brigade that the Army Council are satisfied that the incident which has arisen in regard to their resignations has been due to a misunderstanding.

'It is the duty of all soldiers to obey lawful commands given to them through the proper channel by the Army Council, either for the protection of public property and the support of the civil power in the event of disturbances, or for the protection of the lives and property of the inhabitants.

'This is the only point it was intended to put to the officers in the questions of the General Officer Commanding, and the Army Council have been glad to learn from you that there never has been and never will be any question of disobeying such lawful orders.'

Seely was not present, because he had been sent for by the King. When he did get the draft, the Cabinet had just broken up, and he discussed it with Morley. After this discussion, two further paragraphs were authorized. They read:

'His Majesty's Government must retain their right to use all the forces of the Crown in Ireland, or elsewhere, to maintain law and order and to support the civil power in the ordinary execution of its duty.

'But they have no intention whatever of taking advantage of the right to crush political opposition to the policy or principles of the Home Rule Bill.'

How so experienced a draftsman as Morley came to approve such an unusual written undertaking from the civil power to army officers under its control is to be explained by the heat and haste of the moment. Morley admitted, a day or two later in the House of Lords, that the drafting had been done with his aid.

Far though these paragraphs went, they did not go far enough for Gough. He, on having been handed the whole undertaking with its five paragraphs, asked to be given a quarter of an hour to consider it with the colonels. French was upset, and said that the King was waiting for him to know if all had been settled. Gough and the colonels again had their way, and were not satisfied that the phrase 'crush political opposition' was sufficiently definite. It was, they feared, ambiguous, and might mean anything. Gough records that 'as we were determined that we would not allow ourselves to be exposed again, nor permit our officers and men to be exposed to the contingency of waging civil war on Ulster, and that rather than do so we would prefer to leave the army immediately, and as it was important to have our attitude clearly defined we wrote out what we took to be the meaning of the last phrase'.

They returned with this addition to the already swollen documentation, and showed it to French. The question put to him and Ewart was, 'In the event of the present Home Rule Bill becoming law, can we be called upon to enforce it on Ulster under the expression of maintaining law and order?' Gough required a categorical assurance that what he had already received in writing meant that the answer to his question was in the negative. French said, 'That seems all right'. He walked up and down the room once or twice, considering the point and then, without further remark, sat down at the table and wrote under Gough's signature, 'That is how I read it. J. F.' Having thus secured as extraordinary a blank cheque as a general has ever been given, Gough bade farewell to French and Ewart and departed to catch the night mail for Ireland.

While all this drafting and signing was in process, the House met to begin the first of a series of furious debates on what was variously to be defined as the 'Curragh Mutiny' and the 'Pogrom Plot'. The ministry came at once under fire from two sides; the Opposition attacked it for having tried to use the armed forces of the Crown to provoke loyal Ulstermen to violence so as to have an excuse for shooting them down. From the ministerial side of the House came criticism no less vehement of the playboy cavalry soldiers who had allowed their political views to get the better of their sense of discipline. What Paget had said, and more than even he could possibly have said, was freely quoted. Bonar Law came armed with letters from serving officers and argued from them that much more than merely protective operations had been planned. Balfour accused Asquith of having intended to coerce Ulster and then shrinking from doing so.

Ramsay MacDonald said that the Syndicalists, who had failed to poison the Labour Party with their doctrines, had apparently succeeded with the Tories. John Ward, a Labour member from the Potteries, denounced the officers for having thrown over their allegiance to the King. He read a Syndicalist manifesto, published that day, to the men of the British Army, urging them to remember that officers had exercised an option as to obeying orders, and asking them to resolve that they would never fire a shot against their own class. Mr. J. H. Thomas, the Labour member from Derby, warned the House that his union had given notice to the railway companies in the name of 400,000 workers, which would expire on November 1. He would do his best to effect an amicable settlement but, if the Opposition doctrine held good, his duty would be to tell the railwaymen to organize their forces and to spend the union's half million of capital in providing arms and ammunition. When, in the evening, Ward was taken as a guest into the smoking-room of the National Liberal Club, he was enthusiastically cheered for, as one member put it, 'saying what we all think'.

The two conflicting views of the situation — that there had been a wicked plot and that the cavalry officers had gone on strike — continued through the next few weeks bitterly to divide the nation.

Gough and the colonels were received in triumph at the Curragh. All ranks turned out and they were loudly cheered as they drove along the road through the camp. One non-commissioned officer has described it as the 'grand reception we gave our returning heroes'. Gough spoke a few words before entering his quarters, claiming that they all had the same right as other men, in spite of the fact of their being soldiers, to follow the dictates of their conscience.

What would nowadays be called a 'fan mail' reached Gough in the next few days from all over the country. It has survived in a red bound volume. The majority of writers were on his side. 'The country owes you a great deal for putting this rotten government in their places' wrote a correspondent who signed himself 'A Civilised Welshman'. 'All praise to you and to the noble men who followed your example' came from 'M. A., Cambridge'. Others wrote: 'Accept the thanks of an old soldier for the grand stand you have made for the honour of the service. I was always proud of my red jacket, but never more so than today'; 'I am only a railway clerk, but let me tell you how the men at Derby appreciate your conduct. We may be Radicals but we are Protestants first. Bravo. As officers (gentlemen) you have saved the army. An officer in the Cavalry Brigade can be *trusted* and *respected for ever.*'

A minority of the writers were bitter in their condemnation. 'Several Bournemouth working men' wrote, 'You are a disgrace to your King and country and horse whipping would be too good for you and all who have degraded the flag'. An anonymous letter from Paris read, 'Either you are a knave or a *coward*, certainly not a soldier, for he is supposed to be *brave*. I am an officer myself and always understood that a *gentlemanly* soldier (not a cheap politician) should *bravely* obey orders from the King's existing government. You are a disgrace to any army.' The violence and the vulgarity of these conflicting extracts are an indication of how widely tempers had been lost.

Fergusson, whose patient and resolute diplomacy has been described, found himself in trouble both from the King and in Parliament. Lord Stamfordham wrote to him saying that the King was much disturbed by a letter he had seen from one of the infantry colonels, which contained the statement that the reason why his battalion had decided to carry on was that Fergusson had given them the assurance of the General Officer Commanding-in-Chief that what was ordered had been fully approved by His Majesty. The colonel's letter had included the phrase, 'The King has given the order and we one and all obeyed'.

Fergusson replied explaining that he had acted under the firm impression that he was carrying out 'both technically and in reality the order of His Majesty'. Fergusson further told Stamfordham, 'I have been deceived and have deceived the officers and men under, my command. In honour, and apart from personal inclinations, there is no course open to me but to resign my appointment.' But the King, on hearing the full details of Fergusson's activities, had a telegram sent, telling the General 'most certainly do nothing' and following it up with another Stamfordham letter saying, 'Of course you were perfectly right, considering what you were told, to do as you did'.

Wilson, who had been having the time of his life seeing Bonar Law, Milner, Gwynne (the Editor of the *Morning Post*) and other interested Conservatives to whom he told everything he really knew, was delighted with the turn of events. Determined that there should be no weakening, he sent words of encouragement to Gough: 'I wired Hubert at midnight to stand like a rock. This is vital. Any false move now on our part would be fatal. So long as we hold the paper we got on Monday, we can afford to sit tight.' They could indeed, for the forces on their side were strong and convinced of righteousness.

As the Government fenced to avoid giving full details of its frustrated plans, belief grew stronger and stronger in a plot. Almost every day up to Easter saw some new development. The text of the 'peccant paragraphs', as they quickly came to be called, and the written gloss put upon them by French became known without delay. Seely offered to resign, but Asquith told him that this was unnecessary. Asquith in the Commons and Morley in the Lords stated that the paragraphs were no longer to be regarded as operative. Asquith described them as being really innocuous though capable of being read 'in different senses'. But he came down with a hammer-blow on the written exchanges between Gough and French. What Gough had written, with French's endorsement of it, amounted to 'a new claim which, if allowed, would place the Government and the country at the mercy of the army'. The Government, said Asquith, would never yield to the claim of any body of men in the service of the Crown to demands in advance of what they would or would not be required to do in circumstances that had not arisen. This may not unfairly be described as shutting the door after the horse has got out into the field.

Its immediate consequence was to cause French and Ewart to resign. Efforts were made behind the scenes to persuade them to withdraw their resignations. Haldane, working on the old friendship he had made at the War Office, saw them and wrote a long letter to Asquith seeking to persuade him that military resignations were unnecessary. Asquith stuck to his guns. Seely made a second offer of resignation, and this time it was accepted. Asquith became his own War Minister, declaring, a few days later, that 'the army will hear nothing of politics from me and, in return, I expect to hear nothing of politics from the army'. It was a wise move — indeed, almost the

M

only wise move that had so far been made. The soldiers trusted Asquith; his massive common sense and refusal to be stampeded into the excitement of the moment proved invaluable. The resignations proceeded to the accompaniment of a running commentary from both sides of both Houses. Morley dismissed the plot as being no more than a 'sinister hallucination' and toyed with the idea of resignation, because of his share in the matter of the paragraphs. But he did not resign.

Haldane got himself into trouble through a flagrant alteration in his own speech before it appeared in Hansard. He had informed their Lordships that 'No orders were issued, no orders are likely to be issued, no orders will be issued for the coercion of Ulster'. When he came to look at this at the proof stage, he felt that these words might be misunderstood, and so he inserted 'immediate' before 'coercion'. The change was noticed because of the difference between the press reports of his speech and the amended version of it in Hansard. Haldane's difficulty at that point was shared by all his colleagues. They hoped to avoid making public more than the barest particulars of what Seely and Churchill had planned. The Opposition was quite determined to extract the whole story from them.

A White Paper, issued on March 25, contained a meagre selection of documents and telegrams, but had nothing whatever about the fleet orders. A month was to elapse before another and a much fuller White Paper was extracted. The natural consequence of this reticence was to encourage credulity. Politicians and many ordinary citizens so worked themselves up that they were persuaded that ministers really had desired to provoke bloodshed.

The Prime Minister's wife, Margot, wrote a frantic appeal to Austen Chamberlain. 'Do you realize', she asked, 'where we should have been now if there *had been* a "plot" to overwhelm Ulster with millions of men and ships. We should have been *swept* out by every back bench Liberal and the whole public opinion of this island. I will go further; the first shot that is fired now my Henry goes down and all his life's work is over. *There never* was "a plot" of any sort or kind, I swear, as I wish God to help me both here and hereafter.'

But Mrs. Asquith was playing for once the role of Mrs. Partington. The tide of allegations swept on. Before she dispatched her *cri de cœur*, a remarkable manifestation had been given of how large sections of the British public were rallying to the Ulster cause.

CHAPTER XII

WEST END CLUBMEN ON PARADE

ON Saturday, April 4, fourteen platforms were erected in Hyde Park to form an immense circle between the Serpentine and the Bayswater Road. Thither processions from twenty-two different rendezvous approached. The object of the demonstration was to gain assent to this resolution: 'We protest against the use of the army and the navy to drive out by force of arms our fellow subjects in Ireland from their full heritage in the Parliament of the United Kingdom. And we demand that the Government shall immediately submit this grave issue to the people.'

The composition of the converging processions was such that it is hard to think of an historical parallel. Members of the Carlton, Junior Carlton, Conservative, Constitutional and Junior Constitutional Clubs marched together in one column. *The Times* reporter noted that they formed 'a sombre but dignified parade of silk hats and black coats'. Peers, ex-Cabinet Ministers, Members of Parliament and the English and Scottish Chief Unionist Whips were there. So was the Ladies' Imperial Club, every lady carrying a Union Jack. Members of the British League for the Support of Ulster divided itself into guards for each of the platforms. The drill learnt so effectively in Belfast was now being carried out in London.

The city contingents, representing the Stock Exchange, Lloyds, Mincing Lane and other centres, united their forces at Charing Cross. Bands playing patriotic tunes swept through the streets from the seventy-six con-

stituencies forming Greater London. Working men and
their womenfolk came in brakes. What struck *The Times*
reporter even more than the formal processions was 'the
unceasing trend of individuals to the Marble Arch and
Hyde Park Corner. The quiet middle-class man may be
a little shy of marching through the West End in a column
of route, but not even the menace of a drenching afternoon,
which happily was not realized, deterred him from mounting
the little red, white and blue badge inscribed "Support
Loyal Ulster", carrying the British flag in his hand and
making his way to his selected speaker.' The Union Jack
was everywhere. It flew from windows and on omnibuses,
motors, bicycles, costers' barrows and the dustcart of a
road-sweeper.

The 'quiet middle-class man' and his not so quiet
neighbours had a bumper choice of speakers. But before
they could be heard the Carson technique of whipping up
enthusiasm at a mass meeting came into play. Carson,
who carried his blackthorn stick, had a great reception
when he mounted the platform. One of the countless
little Union Jacks was handed up to him and he fastened
it in his buttonhole. The proceedings opened with the
singing of 'O God, our help in ages past' and the National
Anthem. An hour later a body of buglers from the
Veterans' Club sounded a call and, after a moment's pause,
a roar of voices acclaimed the resolution.

Each orator faced westwards owing to the direction of
the wind; it was the era before the coming of loud-speakers.
The Conservative statesmen who spoke included Austen
Chamberlain, Milner, Walter Long, F. E. Smith, Londonderry and two exceedingly rare migrants in Hyde Park —
Robert Cecil and Balfour. The crowd struck up 'For he's
a jolly good fellow' as, to its huge delight, Balfour mounted
a narrow bench on the lorry which did duty as a platform.
His speech was cut short owing to the competition of
reverberating cheers from the neighbouring platforms. He

was, he explained, making his first, and probably his last, speech in Hyde Park.

Robert Cecil told his section of the audience that he did not know what was in the 'dark and tortuous' mind of Churchill, but he did know that he 'contemplated the slaughter of hundreds of thousands of his fellow men'. At the mention of the name of the First Lord of the Admiralty, there were cries of 'blackguard'. Near by, Lord Charles Beresford was, in his breezy, quarter-deck style, describing the First Lord as 'a Lilliput Napoleon, a man with an unbalanced mind, an egomaniac'.

The afternoon was a triumph, in spite of two jarring notes. The police had to prevent a militant suffragist counter-demonstration and to arrest Mrs. Drummond. A Labour demonstration was held in Trafalgar Square to protest against the different treatment of politicians and officers on the one hand, and of anti-militarist strike leaders and suffragettes on the other. The Labour resolution, which was surely read with mixed feelings in the cavalry mess at the Curragh, approved the conduct of the officers and urged the rank and file to refuse to take up arms against their own class in industrial disputes.

It must have been a self-denying ordinance that kept Wilson from speaking at this rally; but the day was not an idle one for him. He spent an hour with Milner, and expatiated on the vital importance of making the Government explain what orders they gave to Paget. 'The disclosure of these orders will absolutely abolish the cry of "the people versus the army", and will ruin Winston Churchill, Lloyd George, Birrell, Seely and (I think) Asquith.'

During the first week of April the House debated the second reading of the Home Rule Bill, and repeated attempts were made to get at the facts which, if made public, would, Wilson and his political friends hoped, ruin ministers. But, in spite of angry interchanges, a rather

more sober note prevailed. Balfour expressed the sentiments of all except the extremists when he said that what
was in everybody's thoughts was not the merits or the
demerits of the Bill, 'but how with decent credit to ourselves, we can avoid the national calamity of civil war'.
He referred to the marvellous change in the temper of the
House, and asked, 'Does that mean that we are agreed?',
candidly answering his own question with 'No, it means
we are frightened'.

The soldiers at least were settling down. Sir Charles
Douglas had been appointed C.I.G.S. in place of French,
and Sir Henry Sclater took over from Ewart as Adjutant-
General. A new Army Order had been issued as part of
Asquith's attempt to restore military equilibrium. Its
text was as follows:

'No officer or soldier should in future be questioned by
his superior officer as to the attitude he will adopt or as to
his action in the event of his being required to obey orders
dependent on future or hypothetical contingencies.

'An officer or soldier is forbidden in future to ask for
assurances as to orders which he may be required to obey.

'In particular it is the duty of every officer and soldier
to obey all lawful commands given to them through the
proper channel, either for the safeguarding of public
property, or the support of the civil power in the ordinary
execution of its duty, or for the protection of the lives and
property of the inhabitants in the case of disturbance of
the peace.'

Even Carson showed some slight willingness to help
towards a settlement. He offered to submit to Ulster a
proposal, if the Government would agree, leaving Parliament to determine what should happen after the end of
six years. But he continued to stand firmly against
automatic inclusion at the end of six years, and the Government would not meet him. The Bill got its second reading
by a majority of eighty.

Outside the House, Seely told a meeting at Ilkeston that he did not propose to appear in a white sheet. The Conservative members had gone mad and thought that there was a plot to overwhelm Ulster by force of arms. So wicked a plan could not have been thought of by any Government, least of all a Liberal Government. This did not silence his critics, who continued with their accusations and demands over Easter.

Two German professors provided an interlude by writing a letter which was published in *The Times* on Good Friday. (Newspapers did not, at that period, cease publication on Good Fridays.) The joint signatories, Kuno Meyer and Theodor Schiemann, attacked the 'hope and belief' expressed by Ulster Covenanters, that 'in the case of Home Rule becoming law, Germany might be induced to interfere in the cause of Protestantism in Ulster'. They quoted from a leaflet 'distributed under the eye of Sir Edward Carson', which had included this passage: 'If the Home Rule Bill is passed, we shall consider ourselves absolutely justified in asking and rendering every assistance at the first opportunity to the greatest Protestant nation on earth, Germany, to come over and help us.'

The professors continued: 'The amazing delusion that such an appeal would find sympathy and perhaps response is another proof of the fact that the Covenanters live wholly in the ideas and sentiments of a bygone age. We fear Ulster will wait in vain for another William to come to her defence. . . . Today it is no longer a question of Protestantism versus Catholicism or vice versa. The great modern principle of religious equality has in every civilized nation superseded those antiquated and bigoted ideas of hostility and exclusion. No civilized country, least of all Germany, could look favourably on any policy which would run counter to the spirit of religious comprehension.'

Carson spent the days immediately after this Teutonic

rebuke had been delivered having another of his inspection
tours of his armed forces. As he finished, the propagandist
guns of Ulster set down another barrage. On April 17
the Ulster Unionist Council issued a long document pur-
porting to give the 'actual facts' of the 'plan of campaign',
which Paget had been ordered to put into effect. Details
were given in this document of how troops, including
some 10,000 from Lichfield and Aldershot, were to march
into Ulster with naval support. The Belfast police, it was
stated, were to have taken forcible possession of the Old
Town Hall at Belfast — an action that would, inevitably,
have resulted in bloodshed.

    Fortified by this, Bonar Law, in the House, pressed for
a judicial enquiry ; Asquith refused it. There was uproar,
Unionists shouting 'We want your statement on oath' and
'Running away !' Bonar Law asked, 'Will the Prime
Minister kindly tell us why, if there is nothing to be
ashamed of, he objects to having the truth tested where the
statements are given on oath and can be established ?'

    Asquith for once allowed himself to display indignation.
He raised his hand and brought it down with a loud rap on
the dispatch box, vehemently exclaiming, 'That, Sir, is an
imputation against the honour of ministers'. Bonar Law
returned to the charge. Asquith, with lips compressed and
gathered brows, brought his fist down on the dispatch box
more loudly than before. Bonar Law had the last words :
'I have already accused the Prime Minister of making
statements which are false,' he said in deliberate tones,
'and he has refused to take an opportunity of either explaining or withdrawing them'.

    The Government yielded to these pressures to the
extent of issuing a second White Paper, containing far
more information than had its predecessor. This time they
included a section of fleet orders and a written statement by
Paget. Ministers had been in correspondence with him
and brought him over to London in their efforts to get

some sort of coherent account of what he thought he had
said to his officers. It was a Herculean task, and its fruits
now published only confirmed suspicions of his muddle-
headedness and of the rashness, to put it mildly, of those
who helped him. He admitted that he had said that 'I
thought that the moves would create intense excitement,
and that the country, — and if not the country, then the
Press — would be ablaze on the following day. I said that
the moves might possibly lead to opposition, and might
even eventuate, and in the near future, in the taking of
active operations against organized bodies of the Ulster
Volunteer Force under their responsible leaders.' He also
admitted that 'the most I had been able to obtain from
Colonel Seely, and that only at a late hour, and by the help
of Sir John French', was the concession for officers actually
domiciled in Ulster. Some officers, he thought, had
understood him 'completely', but others 'understood me
to mean that any officer who was not prepared, from
conscientious or other motives, to carry out his duty was to
say so, and would then be dismissed from the Service.

'I do not understand now how the misconception
arose in all cases, but Brigadier-General Forestier-Walker
(one of the officers who shared the misapprehension)
informs me that, not seeing why Colonel Seely should hope
that there would be very few cases of officers claiming
exemption owing to a domicile in Ulster, he jumped
erroneously to the conclusion that I had made a slip in
quoting Colonel Seely's remark and that the latter had
really meant that he hoped that there would be very few
cases of officers who would be dismissed from the Army
rather than do their duty.

'It is easy to see that from this it would be a natural
step to infer that something in the nature of an alternative
was to be put to officers.

'Be that as it may, certain officers did leave the conference under a wrong impression.' He ended with, 'I

regret extremely that this misapprehension arose, and I alone am responsible for it.'

Paget's confused testimony added little to the information already garnered by the Opposition from so many other first-hand sources; they refused to believe either that he was accurate or that the White Paper had told everything. They submitted Asquith to a savage cross-examination to explain how he had come to make that reticent statement to *The Times* (quoted above on p. 151) when, as the White Paper now showed, far more ambitious fleet movements had been ordered. Asquith, with his usual skill, sought to reconcile what he had said and what he had not said to *The Times*. There had been, he explained, a general permission given by the Cabinet on March 11 to move a battle squadron from Arosa Bay to Lamlash, but he (Asquith) had not known that this was being acted upon until he heard about it from Churchill on the Saturday of 'mutiny' week. He had promptly modified the arrangements of his First Lord and so his interview in *The Times* was accurate. He agreed that an Opposition motion of enquiry into the whole affair should be debated on the following Tuesday and Wednesday, April 28 and 29.

It was to be a tremendous oratorical battle, but before it began, the Ulstermen had brought off a spectacular *coup*. During Friday night and the early hours of Saturday morning, April 24 and 25, a major operation in gunrunning was successfully carried out.

CHAPTER XIII

THE *FANNY* GETS THE GUNS

DURING those politically mad March days, a little tramp steamer, the *Fanny* (to give her the first of the several names under which she sailed), was bucking to and fro in the seas between Germany and Ireland. The Ulstermen had on hand a more daring and ambitious project than that of raiding the arms stores, the defence of which was getting Seely, Churchill and the Generals into such heavy water. Loud though they were in their protestations of being prepared to go to all lengths, Carson, Craig and the rest might never have plunged into the adventure of gun-running on so large a scale had they not been encouraged to do so by as remarkable a little man as any of the characters in this narrative.

Frederick Hugh Crawford had, in 1914, reached his early fifties and could look back on a colourful experience of gun-running which stretched into the 'nineties. He was a member of one of the oldest Presbyterian families in the north. He had been one of the twenty men who signed the Covenant with their own blood and he claimed that, in so doing, he followed a tradition started by an ancestor who had done the same at the signing of the Scottish Solemn League and Covenant in 1738. Several of his ancestors were ministers, and he had received his education at the Methodist College in Belfast. After serving as a premium apprentice in the great shipbuilding firm of Harland & Wolff, he had roamed the world and returned — with an interval of fighting in South Africa — to throw himself into the thick of the anti-Home Rule fight.

He was no orthodox fighter. His ingenious brain had worked out a plot to kidnap Gladstone on the Brighton front and to maroon him, as at St. Helena, in a Pacific island. Crawford's fervent wish to see the back of Mr. Gladstone was combined with a certain consideration for the old gentleman. The kidnapping arrangements included the provision of Homer, the Bible, writing-paper and an axe for felling palm trees, thus allowing for the indulgence of all the Liberal Prime Minister's hobbies. Unfortunately for the gaiety of journalists at the time, and of future historians, Lord Ranfurly refused to advance the £10,000 needed for this enterprise.

Crawford then turned his attention to acquiring an extensive and peculiar knowledge of the international gun market. He had some successes in smuggling arms into Ulster, and some setbacks. The one that saddened him most occurred at Hammersmith, where, with the kindly aid of a member of Parliament, he had, in 1913, made a hoard of rifles, hidden in a warehouse store. But disturbing news reached him from his Hammersmith agent. A police guard had been put on the rifles. He hurried to London and saw his solicitors, Messrs. Lewes & Lewes. They made enquiries and were informed by the Home Secretary that a Victorian Act of Parliament prohibited the importation of gun-barrels which had not been tested by the London and Birmingham Gunmakers' Guild. The penalty for infringement was a fine of £2 a barrel or prison. The Act did not apply to Ireland but, alas, the gun-barrels had not yet crossed to Ireland. So Crawford, as he sadly recalled, had been 'dished'. It meant that, 'if I claim the rifles I shall be liable to a penalty of £15,000 and, in addition, I would have to come into the open'.

This and other lessons were not lost on him. By the time he appealed to Carson for support, in 1914, for his most daring exploit, he was already a professional in the gun-running game. Happily he was more than a remarkable man of action; he could write vividly and he has left a spirited account of his own exploits. He explained to Carson how, through the connexion he had built up in Germany, he was hopeful of being able to arm the Volunteers on an ample and up-to-date scale. But he made no bones about the dangers. 'Those who back me up,' he told Carson, 'must run the risk equally with me of imprisonment. Are you willing to back me to the finish in this undertaking? If you are not, I do not go; but if you are, I shall go even if I know I will not return. It is for Ulster and her freedom that I am working, and that alone.'

Crawford continues: 'I so well remember the scene. We were alone. Sir Edward was sitting opposite to me. When I had finished his face was stern and grim, there was a glint in his eyes which I had not seen before. He rose to his full height, looking me in the eyes, and advanced to where I was sitting. He stared down at me, shook his fist in my face, and in a steady and determined voice which thrilled through me, said, "Crawford, I'll see you through this business, even if I should have to go to prison for it".'

'I rose from my chair and holding out my hand to him, said, "Sir Edward, that is all I want. I leave tonight."'

On arrival in Hamburg he saw one Spiro, a Jew in whom he had, with good reason, complete trust. They arranged to take delivery of a consignment of twenty thousand modern rifles. Crawford was a great believer in getting every detail right. He insisted that one rifle and one hundred rounds of ammunition must be wrapped up and five rifles packed together with straw-packing so that they would be ready for instant use and easy handling when unloaded. This was a prudent move, for he was afterwards able to boast that 'I anticipated both military and police attempts to stop the cargo coming ashore and I knew our men would run any risk rather than loose their rifles'. While the packing was being done, Crawford passed to and fro between Hamburg and Belfast, keeping in touch with the Ulster leaders who were, by now, all supporting him.

The next move was to get a ship. Arrangements were made with the director of an Antrim company for one of its sea captains, Andy Agnew, to accompany Crawford on a continental tour of inspection. Early in March they chose the *Fanny*. She could only steam at eight knots, but seemed otherwise suitable, and they promptly closed on her at £2000. Crawford conducted these negotiations as an American, calling himself John Washington Graham of New York, and assuming an appropriate accent. The *Fanny* having been secured, the next difficulty was to decide about ownership. 'I did not want the *Fanny* to be confiscated by the British Government after capture by a warship, and I intended to sail her under the Norwegian flag.' This was done by getting the Norwegian captain to take over the vessel as his own and to give Crawford a mortgage on her for sixty thousand marks.

The contraband cargo had to be got into her hold. Crawford and his associates spent long hours pondering how to bring this off. 'No one will ever realize what all the worry and anxiety meant to Spiro, Schneider and myself. Schneider was eventually worn to a shadow.' While Spiro and Crawford were talking matters over in a restaurant, the latter suddenly heard a voice say, 'Go with the guns tonight and don't lose sight of them until you have handed them over in Ulster'. He gave a start and asked Spiro if he had spoken. Spiro denied that he had, but the voice repeated those words four times. Encouraged by this evidence of supernatural backing, Crawford took the plunge and set off down the river Elbe.

His tug flew a black flag, which he was informed would indicate to all pilots that they had the right of way. At Kiel there was an alarm. The Master told them that three men had come on board and tried to find out where they were going and what was their cargo. These men were assumed to be Mexicans, for some dissident citizens of that republic were known to be competing in the arms market with Ulster. When Churchill had made his reference to Britain being reduced to a Mexican level, he was speaking more plainly than he knew.

More serious than these competitors was the arrival of a German official who said that they could not sail because he believed that they had rifles in the lighters. Voluminous papers were produced without satisfying authority. Schneider turned to Crawford and said, 'This man is going to cause trouble'. Crawford, who spoke no German, replied, 'Give him some money'. Schneider put a hundred mark note into his hand. The official looked at it, smiled, glided it into his pocket and said, 'I see that your papers are in order and shall detain you no longer. Good night.' It was, perhaps, as well for him that he did, for Crawford records that 'Had the official insisted on detaining us, I would have taken him below and not released him until the *Fanny* sailed'.

The Danish port officer proved more intractable when the cargo had been brought to the *Fanny*. Her manifest described it as 'general' and showed that she was bound from Bergen to Iceland. The port officer was not satisfied, and unmoved by attempted bribery. He took their papers away for examination, promising to return them later that evening. They hurried on with the loading and then, in three hours' time, saw a motor-launch approaching with other Danish officers. A man 'with a face like a ferret' came aboard and said that he wanted to examine the cargo. These unwelcome visitors departed after asking a series of questions which could not satisfactorily be answered, and they took away with them all the papers.

Crawford 'felt like a rat caught in a trap. If we decided to run the gauntlet, we had to pass a torpedo boat station in the channel, which was only navigable within about a mile and a half from the naval base. We were sure to be stopped, because the naval base had certainly been warned about us. Even now I shrink from the mental agony that I suffered at that time. What would the Ulster Volunteers think when they heard of this naked failure to deliver the guns after all the promises made to them time and again from every Unionist platform in Ulster? Had we been captured by a man-of-war or sunk when resisting capture, there might have been some glory in the enterprise.

'But to be tamely trapped without a blow being struck! To be brought into a naval base and to lie there while the whole Ulster plot was being unravelled and made known to the world as a ghastly failure, the leaders the laughing stock of the world! The thought of it caused the sweat to pour off me in an agony of remorse and disappointment. I walked up and down the deck, tormented by the thought of all those men waiting for me to bring them the weapons with which to fight for their religion, their liberty and all that was dear to them. I went into my cabin and threw myself on my knees, and in simple language told God all about it: what this meant to Ulster, that there was nothing sordid in what we desired, that we wanted nothing selfishly. I pointed out all this to God and thought of the old psalm, "O God, our help in ages past, our hope for years to come".'

Emerging from this vigil, Crawford heard from the defeatist Schneider that the men wanted to cease loading but, fortified by his appeal to the Almighty, the little ringleader offered to double the wages and the men set to work again with a will. At daybreak, it seemed that Providence was indeed on the Orange side. 'I arose,' says Crawford, 'and the sight I saw gladdened my heart. It was blowing half a gale and there was a low mist on the water, restricting visibility to some three or four hundred yards. I called to Agnew to shorten sail and to be ready to weigh at a moment's notice. I went back to my cabin and fell on my knees and if ever true thankfulness was expressed in prayer it was that morning by me.'

N

They would beat the Danish authorities yet, but another shock was to come. 'I heard the engines being reversed and old Falke (the Norwegian skipper) dancing and shouting like a monkey on a stick. I looked over the side and there before me was a willow stick marking the shallows. In a moment the previous night's black horror seized me again. My eyes remained fascinated by the willow stick. If we ran aground, our last state was worse than our first. We were technically pirates and could be hanged. At last I realized that the willow was slowly receding from us and that we were safe.'

They wormed the *Fanny* out of the channel with mud churning up all round them, passed the naval base and reached the open sea. As soon as they were clear, all hands were turned on to cutting off the iron letters on the funnel, changing the colour and repainting the name on the bows and stern. For *Fanny* was substituted *Bethia*, the name of Crawford's youngest daughter.

It was one thing to get clear of the Continent and another to reach Ireland through the British fleet. Looking in at Trelleborg, they saw a newspaper which carried a report about the mysterious ship *Fanny* and her load of rifles and ammunition. While they were wondering what to do next, Crawford had one of the crew paint 'Anvers' instead of 'Bergen' on the stern of the now *Bethia*. Then he went down with an attack of malaria. A gale sprang up, and heavy seas shattered the glass of the lamp so that they could only show a port light and, after two or three nights, they knew by the erratic manœuvring of other ships that they must, at all costs, call at the nearest port and get a new glass. They put into Great Yarmouth late one evening, and Agnew went ashore to buy a new starboard light and then to go on to London to make arrangements for another steamer to meet the *Fanny* alias the *Bethia* at Lundy Island on the following Friday or Saturday so that the cargo might be transhipped.

Meanwhile, the *Bethia* set course for the English Channel, changing her name again for that of Crawford's second daughter, Doreen. They steamed out of territorial waters; then Crawford had a return attack of malaria and could eat nothing. When they were off Dunkirk, Falke came into his cabin and said, 'Mr. Graham, you are very ill. I have sailed for over forty years and I know a sick man when I see one. You have enteric fever and will die in two days if you are not put ashore. I am going to put you ashore.' There was a fierce argument. Crawford ordered Falke to keep on his course till they came to Ushant and then to steer for the Bristol Channel. Falke replied, 'I'm taking you into Dunkirk. You will be dead soon. You have eaten nothing for a long time and no man can live without eating.' 'Captain Falke, I am not a dead man by any means. Are you going to obey me or not?' 'No, I am taking you into Dunkirk.'

Crawford went to a drawer in his cabin and took out a ·38 colt automatic pistol and put it to Falke's head, saying, 'Captain Falke, I know I am alone amongst you and your foreign crew, but I am a match for all of you if you attempt to interfere with my orders. I will shoot you, or any of your crew who interferes, as dead as a herring. I ask you for the last time, will you obey my orders?' 'I will, I will.' 'Shake hands. Now leave me, please.' After this, if Crawford's memory is to be relied upon — and there is no reason to suppose that it is not — he and Falke were the best of friends. Falke even tried cooking to tempt Crawford to eat. 'He told me afterwards that in all his sea experience he had never sailed with two such men as Agnew and me, and I don't think he ever wanted to again.'

Up the Bristol Channel they went, beset with pilot boats coming to offer their services. But these were the last people with whom they wanted to have anything to do. Pilots, in Crawford's view, 'are notoriously inquisitive'. They dodged them 'without appearing to do so'.

They seemed to come down like a flight of locusts; fortunately they were all sailing-boats and not motor. Another tax on the nerves of the gun-runners was that a number of trawlers, all of which appeared to have wireless aboard, 'seemed to be strongly drawn to us'.

The next day, Sunday, and on Sunday night, they stood off from Lundy in a north-westerly direction, giving a signal every ten minutes when no vessels were in sight, and every two or three minutes when lights came in view. At about 5 o'clock in the morning, Falke called Crawford to say that a steamer, the *Balmarino*, had come along with Andy Agnew aboard, but that a fishing-vessel with radio was near by. The two steamers went on for some ten miles to get clear of the fishing-vessel, and then stopped. Agnew came aboard the *Doreen* (to give her transiently current name) and reported that he had been to London and seen Carson and Craig. The situation, he had learnt, was now desperate. There was a threat of Belfast being bombarded by the fleet and a division had been ordered to go over to Ulster from Aldershot. The only ray of light in the darkness was that officers, under Gough, had refused to fight against the loyalists.

Agnew had brought with him the skipper of the *Balmarino* (the little steamer owned by Lord Leitrim), who presented a letter. This instructed Crawford to return to the Baltic and to cruise there for three months, 'keeping in touch with the Committee during that time'. When he read those words, they seemed to Crawford 'to sear into my brain as with a red-hot iron'. There were no signatures. 'I did not wonder at that; I gave them the credit of being too much ashamed of their action to put their names to such a cowardly document. After the hell of anxieties which I had suffered, I could not understand these instructions, in spite of what Agnew told me of the situation. If the British Government had thrown down the gage of battle to Ulster, was it not all the more reason

why we should be armed to resist the threatened coercion?'
Crawford did not need to think twice about how to dismiss
this Quisling missive. He ordered the skipper of the
Balmarino to go back to the person or persons who had
sent him and to 'tell them to go to hell', and he added, to
make sure that they understood that he meant business,
'if I do not receive an official document with instructions
for landing my cargo within the next six days, I shall run the
ship aground in Ballyholme Bay at high water and rouse the
County Down Volunteers to come and take her cargo off'.

Crawford was shrewd as well as pugnacious, and he
realized that this situation needed delicate handling. It
would, he felt, be too much to hope that the now notorious
Fanny would be allowed to dock unmolested at an Irish
port; another vessel, preferably a harmless coal-boat,
must carry the guns on their last lap. He landed at Tenby,
where another of those prying customs officers interrogated
him at some length, and then set off to catch the Irish mail
train to Rosslare. There another customs officer 'found
a Colt automatic in my possession and seized it, but I
succeeded in getting to Dublin in time to catch the train
for Belfast'.

He was taken to Craigavon, where his host, Craig, 'held
out his hand, but I did a cruel thing: I swept his hand
aside and regretted it the same moment. I said, "I will
shake hands with no member of the Committee until I
know what they propose to do with the *Fanny*'s cargo".
Instead of being offended, Craig put his arm round
Crawford and said, "It's all right, Fred, the Chief is here".'
In a short time the Committee came in. Crawford was
still sulky. 'I had little inclination to acknowledge the
greetings which they gave me.' Then Carson came in and
'took my hand in his two, saying, "Well done, Crawford,
I am proud of you".' The old Blarney, exported from
Dublin to Belfast, worked. 'When he said this, I felt
fully rewarded for what I had done.'

They then went into committee, Crawford promptly putting his cards on the table. 'You are breaking your promise to the whole of Ulster, but I shall not break mine, and I refuse to do your dirty work. Gentlemen, I want you to understand me. I will *not* take those guns back.' They asked him what he proposed to do. He explained that the *Fanny* was to meet him off the Tuskar Light next Friday night. (It was a Tuesday.) He wanted to buy a British steamer into which to tranship the cargo and then to bring the guns to Larne. The prudent Richardson feared that it would not be possible to tranship in open water. Crawford swept this objection aside. 'Gentlemen, I have promised nothing so far that I have not carried out. I promise you that I can do this, and it shall be done.' Carson saw that he was face to face with a bird of his own feather. 'Crawford is right. We had better leave the details to him. I am sure that he will see his way to carry out his plans.' He proceeded to do so.

A ship was known to be in Glasgow in good working order and ready for immediate delivery. She was the *Clydevalley* and would be in Belfast next day with coal. Crawford urged the Committee to let him buy her. Carson supported him, and off Crawford went, delivering as a parting shot at the Committee that he would expect no change of plans 'unless they were signed by Sir Edward Carson personally'.

The *Clydevalley* deal was done. It was arranged that she should proceed to Llandudno Bay and pick up Crawford, who would then start for the Tuskar Light. She was late. Crawford sent an anxious wire. 'What has happened to Mary?' In due course he received a wire back, 'Mary missed train, but will arrive late this evening'. After dark he went down to the beach with his handbag. A strong wind had begun to blow, and the waves had risen. At last he saw the port, starboard and masthead lights of a steamer approaching head on for the shore. He went to the water's edge and signalled with his flash-lamp. He could hear a boat approaching above the roar of the breakers. He tumbled in and, boarding the *Clydevalley*, started off in search of the *Fanny*.

Her whereabouts by this time were distressingly vague. Crawford got himself put ashore at Fishguard, and went up, through London, to Great Yarmouth, where he could see no sign of the *Fanny*. He waited for a telegram. When it was delivered, 'I shut my teeth and went into a passage. I knew that the contents of this telegram would decide whether or not this venture was going to be a success or a failure. I opened the telegram and read "All's well. Breakwater 5 P.M. Tuesday. Agnew".' He caught the night train for Holyhead and duly picked up the *Clydevalley*.

Agnew had wonderful news for him. He had managed, with the help of sixteen transport labourers from Belfast, to shift the cargo from the *Fanny* in less than half the time taken by the Germans. So the *Clydevalley* now had on board the goods to be delivered.

They sailed into a lumpy sea and busied themselves painting on three strips of canvas, about 6 ft. long and 12 ins. broad, the name *Mountjoy*. This was a famous name in Ulster. It was taken, not from Crawford's family Bible, but from the vessel, glorious in Orange history, that had broken the boom across the Foyle when the siege of Derry was raised in the war between William III and James II. The new *Mountjoy*, having sailed round the Isle of Man, set sail for the Copeland Islands off the Ulster coast. There a tender met them, but Crawford refused to have anything to do with her until he was sure that the instructions she brought him came from Carson himself. He was told, 'They *are* signed by Sir Edward'. He was to land the bulk of the rifles at Larne and the rest at Bangor and Donaghadee. At 10.30 on the night of April 24 they reached the landing-stage at Larne.

The little seaport of Larne lies about twenty miles north of Belfast on the Irish Sea. The local Volunteers had been mobilized before 8 o'clock and a procession of motor cars and motor lorries almost three miles long had been formed from the direction of Belfast. Pickets had been posted to see that drivers had the necessary permits. It was, in theory, a routine exercise by the Volunteers, and, equally, a detached historian may be forgiven for suspecting that the police were only in theory supposed to know nothing about it. The good work of unloading the rifles and ammunition was speedily effected and dispatched to destinations as far off as Counties Tyrone and Londonderry. Here and there the local police were surrounded by a superior force. There is no record of resistance and there was only one casualty. The coastguard at Donaghadee, riding his bicycle vigorously to give the alarm, fell dead from a heart attack outside the post office. Had he entered, he would have found the lines dead, for the wires had been earthed by the Volunteers.

The men and women of the Volunteer force who had been training for the past six months in flag-signalling had the night of their lives. They finished the job started so single-mindedly by Crawford, and by the week-end they had got the tools. Carson in London received a telegram of one word — lion. It was the code message telling him that Ulster was now armed. The newspapers came out with special editions. As soon as he heard the news, Roberts rushed round to congratulate Carson. Holding out his hand he said 'Magnificent! Magnificent! Nothing could have been better done; it was a piece of organization that any army in Europe might be proud of.'

So the Field-Marshal greeted the statesman.

Such was the prelude to the parliamentary inquest held by the Conservative leaders into the alleged nefarious activities of Seely and Churchill.

CHAPTER XIV

INQUEST INTO PLOT AND MUTINY

THE baiting of ministers lasted for two days and was begun by Austen Chamberlain. He begged to move that there ought to be a full and impartial enquiry into the serious nature of the naval and military movements recently contemplated by the Government against Ulster. Such an enquiry was, according to the motion to which he spoke, needed because of the incompleteness and inaccuracy in material points of the statements made by ministers and of the continued failure of the Government to deal frankly with the situation. Chamberlain hit hard at Churchill. He had evidently collected an anthology of the more forthright Churchillian utterances. He quoted the First Lord as having said, 'There are worse things than bloodshed, even on an extensive scale', and, of course, he referred to the by then famous words, 'Let us go forward together and put these grave matters to the proof'.

He taunted the ministry for having been so costive in its disclosures. The first White Paper, he remarked, which was supposed to have included every material document, contained eight and 'now we have got from them fifty-five'. He reminded Churchill that he had said that the rejection of the Prime Minister's peace offer 'struck in my heart a note of despair'. Chamberlain's was a probing speech. He sought to show that Churchill in despair had deliberately set out to provoke disorder. Had this pugnacious young minister not stated that 'the first British soldier or coastguard, blue-jacket or Irish Constabulary man who is attacked and killed by an Orangeman will arouse an explosion from the country'? Churchill interrupted him, and so did Carson. Members interrupted Carson, shouting at him 'Behave like a king!' 'You behave like a cad,' retorted Carson. The long-suffering Speaker agreed that this was a most improper expression.

Churchill, in this congenial atmosphere of battle, rose to reply. He went over to the attack. 'So, what we are now witnessing in the House', he began, 'is uncommonly like a vote of censure by the criminal classes on the police.' 'You have not arrested them', a member interpolated. 'Is that the complaint — that we have been too lenient?' Churchill exclaimed, and he proceeded superbly to follow the maxim — when in doubt, abuse the plaintiff's attorney.

'The Conservative party, the party of the comfortable, the wealthy — (Hon. Members: "No, no!") — the party of those who have most to gain by the continuance of the existing social order, here they are committed to naked revolution, committed to a policy of armed violence, and utter defiance of lawfully constituted authority, committed to tampering with the discipline of the Army and the Navy, committed to obstructing highways and telegraphs, to overpowering police, coastguards and Customs officials, committed to smuggling in arms by moonlight, committed to the piratical seizure of ships and to the unlawful imprisonment of the King's servants — the Conservative party as a whole committed to that.' So this tremendous sentence reaches its full stop in Hansard.

'That is their position,' Churchill swept on, 'and all the time while their newspapers are chuckling with nervous glee at each sorry event which is recorded, and while they are hurriedly collecting information as if it was news from Mexico, or some other disturbed area, and bringing out special editions with the utmost satisfaction, all the time that that is going on, let me point out to the Conservative party, and those who are associated with them, that there is in this country a great democracy, millions of whom are forced to live their lives under conditions which leave them stripped of all but the barest necessities, who are repeatedly urged to be patient under their misfortunes, repeatedly urged to wait year after year, and Parliament after Parliament, until, in the due workings of the Constitution, some satisfaction is given to their clamant needs, all the time this great audience is watching and is learning from you, from those who have hitherto called themselves "the party of law and order" how much they care for law, how much they value order when it stands in the way of anything they like!

'If that great audience is watching here at home, what of the great audiences that watch in India. Think of the devastating doctrines of the Leader of the Opposition. The right hon. Gentleman may laugh in a brief leadership of the Conservative party, but he has shattered treasure which greater men than he have guarded for generations. Think what the effect of his doctrines would be applied, let us say, to the people of India or of Egypt. Take his doctrine in regard to the Army — his doctrine of what the officers are entitled to choose or not to choose. He was obliged to carry that further, and to say that the men might choose also. I am not going to push this matter too far, but consider the application of that doctrine to the native officers of the Indian Army, or to the native soldiers of the Indian or Egyptian Army, and you will see that, in his insatiable hunger to get into office he is subverting principles which are absolutely vital to the continued organized government of the British Empire.'

It was magnificent, but it was not an answer to what he and Seely had been planning. Lord Winterton interrupted with, 'Oh, let him go on'. Churchill took this in his stride with, 'It is an infinite encouragement to me that my words can produce a salutary impression, however superficial or transient, upon the Noble Lord'. He

accused the Conservatives of teaching the Irish Nationalists the truth that there was in John Bright's famous
saying that Ireland never gained anything except by force.
Then, switching shrewdly to home politics, he asserted
that the use being made of the Orange army had nothing
to do with Ulster. Its object was to show that if the veto
of the Lords were gone, there still remained the veto of
force. 'It was no longer a question of our coercing Ulster;
it was a question of our preventing Ulster from coercing
us.'

At long last he turned to naval and army movements,
prefacing what he had to say with, 'I am certainly not
going into details of confidential discussions which were
held with Sir Arthur Paget and other generals. . . . I
think it is a very cool request on the part of gentlemen
engaged in planning military operations against the
organized Government of the King — on the part of
gentlemen engaged in arming, as they tell us, a hundred
thousand men with rifles and ammunition, to shoot down
the King's servants — I think it is a very cool request that
they should come forward and ask to be informed what
are the precise military or police measures that will be
adopted against them. Therefore I have not the slightest
intention of going into any of those confidential matters.'

But, he assured the House, 'no movements of any kind
were authorized' beyond those for protecting the arms
depots. Paget had, it was true, been given to understand
that 'large reinforcements would be sent' if he needed
them, but 'I want to know, does anybody dispute the
propriety of that? If British troops marching on the
King's highway were shot down and slain by rebel rifles . . .
it would be the duty, the absolute duty, of the executive
Government to strike back with every man or gun they
could command. . . . Naval officers in plain clothes,
troops taken by sea to avoid going through Belfast, were
only a part of the careful measures which we took to prevent

it being possible to bring armed opposition to bear upon these small bodies or small movements while they were actually in process of completion.'

Finishing this part of his speech, Churchill challenged the Opposition with 'All this talk of civil war has not come from us; it has come from you. For the last two years, we have been forced to listen to a drone of threats of civil war with the most blood-curdling accompaniments and consequences. What did they mean by civil war? Did they really think that if a civil war came, it was to be a war in which only one side was to take action? Did they really believe it was all going to be dashing exploits and brilliant gun-running *coups* on the side of rebellion, and nothing but fiendish plots on the part of the Government?' Rubbing his point home, Churchill concluded the attack with, 'I wish to make it perfectly clear that if rebellion comes, we shall put it down, and if it comes to civil war, we shall do our best to conquer in the civil war. But there will be neither rebellion nor civil war unless it is of your making.'

This 'partisan reply', as its author afterwards called it, was splendidly and dramatically rounded off with an appeal to Carson. Taking up a typewritten paper, he said, 'The right hon. Gentleman, the Member for the University of Dublin [Carson] is running great risks — and no one can deny it — in strife. Why will he not run some risk for peace? The key is in his hands now. . . . Why cannot the right hon. and learned Gentleman say boldly "Give me the Amendments to this Home Rule Bill which I ask for, to safeguard the dignity and the interests of Protestant Ulster, and I in return will use all my influence and good will to make Ireland an integral unit in a federal system." . . . If such language were used, I firmly believe that all that procession of hideous and hateful moves and counter-moves that we have been discussing and are now forced to discuss, and that hateful avenue down which we have looked too long, would give place to a clear and bright prospect.'

Opposition speakers who followed were not to be denied their hopes of getting in at a kill. Lord Charles Beresford, returning to the plot charge, asked why the Admiralty had telegraphed for permission to use field-guns in Ulster 'for exercising men in bad weather'. Beresford argued that this was obviously a code — 'anybody could see through that'. Those guns had been wanted in case there was going to be disturbance in Ulster.

Seely followed to point out that as War Minister he had saved the arms depots from being rushed and to ask whether Carson was responsible for the gun-running. 'Yes', said Carson. Having got this cheerful admission, Seely went on with equal cheerfulness to amplify what his colleague at the Admiralty had said. 'If I am accused of a plot, I go further, and on my own responsibility I said [to Paget], "Not only may you have a force to bring you up to any number of thousands you may require to maintain law and order, but you can have as many more as you find necessary, even to the last man".'

On the next day, Balfour took up the running. Churchill's speech had been made up of 'two wholly dissimilar parts, neither of them relevant to the subject under debate; put up to reply in detail to specific and perfectly clear charges, the First Lord had indulged in an outburst of demagogic rhetoric'. Balfour protested that if the Government was 'wicked enough and insane enough to think that the proper course is to coerce Ulster, then frankly coerce her'. The action taken had been deliberately provocative; 'there is one character disgusting to every policeman and which even the meanest criminal thinks inferior to himself in point of morals, and that character is the *agent provocateur*'.

Churchill sprang up to ask whether Balfour was going to bring forward some evidence in support of that state-

ment.   Balfour said that the evidence had been amply
provided in Churchill's own speech.   He went on to strike
a deeper note.   'The right hon. Gentleman appears to hold
the view,' he said, 'which, so far as I know, has never been
held by responsible British statesmen — at any rate, not
for centuries — that there are no circumstances in which
it is justifiable for a population to resist the Government.
They must be most rare.   Such circumstances in any
reasonable community must be of a kind which could only
occur once in two or three centuries without shattering the
whole fabric of society.   But they may occur ; they have
occurred ; and there has never been any question with
regard to some of us on this side of the House that the
coercion of Ulster, in the sense of compelling Ulster to
leave a free Government under which she is happy, and
put her under a Government which she detests, is one of
those cases.'

Carson, who spoke soon after Balfour, introduced, with
his usual adroitness, a new point.   He claimed that the
trade unionists of Belfast were at his back and that it was
nonsense for Labour members to pretend that the Volunteers were a branch of the Conservative Party.   He quoted
an appeal from Ulster to English trade unionists which ran,
'You have been told by the Radical and Socialist press
that Ulster's resistance to Home Rule is an aristocratic
plot.   This is false. . . . Sir Edward Carson leads us
because we, the workers, the people, the democracy of
Ulster, have chosen him as the champion of our stubborn
determination.'

Bonar Law made a personal apologia, sweeping back
over history to prove that, as a Canadian newcomer, he had
not destroyed Tory tradition.   Language 'quite as strong,
quite as clear, and quite as deserving of being classed as
inciting to Ulster as any language which has been used by
me' had come out of such aristocratic mouths as those of
the Dukes of Devonshire and of Argyll in Gladstone's

Cabinet, and of Lords Randolph Churchill and Salisbury. Going back still further, he quoted Pitt who, as he reminded the House, had employed language which had moved the Attorney-General of that day — 'very different from the right hon. Gentleman who fills that post in the present Government' — to cry out, 'My blood runs cold. The Gentleman sounds the trumpet of rebellion, for which he should be sent to another place.'

After Bonar Law had thus defended the fanfares of himself and his colleagues, Asquith rounded off the debate by expressing 'mild surprise'. The plot was 'a mare's nest'. He did not disassociate himself in any way from his colleagues. They had taken precautions. 'What fools we should have been if we had not done so.' The motion was put and received an inevitable rejection. There was to be no 'full and impartial enquiry'. But the debate had cleared the air. Neither side could, without losing face, cease to continue indulging in displays of verbal aggression. Pugnacity was topical; by one of those small coincidences that reward the researcher, a plea was published, on the same day as the report of Churchill's hard-hitting speech, for the granting of a full blue at Oxford and Cambridge for boxing. Beresford was one of the signatories.

Even now, when the dust of more than forty years has settled on the Hansard of 1914, there are still those who believe in all the allegations against the 'plotters', and it is improbable that readers, hearing this story for the first time, will agree on its rights and wrongs. History is always alive in the sense that it never ceases to be controversial. Was there a plot and was there a mutiny? A mutiny there certainly was, but it is not to be sought for in those few days at the Curragh. It spread over a wider area and a longer space of time. It had begun two or three years earlier at Westminster. That generation of politicians, Conservative and Liberal, brought up in the long-drawn-out Victorian peace, broken by nothing worse than remote,

exciting little wars, had temporarily lost its grip on the
ealities that underlie the efficient enforcement of constitutional power.

Gough and his colonels were not guilty of mutiny;
they did not disobey direct orders. Whether they would
have performed their duty as soldiers more faithfully had
they taken the same line as did Fergusson is a matter of
opinion and not of fact. Mutiny there certainly was at the
War Office, and Wilson was its salesman. His unabashed,
incessant habit of playing politics while holding high rank
in the Service was an inexcusable exhibition of disloyalty.
But the legend that grew up around him magnified the
effectiveness of his intriguing to far beyond its true
proportions. The titbits of information he carried, as
proudly as a dog with a shopping basket in its mouth,
to the Opposition leaders were useful to them in their
campaigning against the Government. The effect of his
behaviour on the morale of more junior officers was bad,
but there is no evidence that it was decisive. He was not
of the metal to lead a mutiny. He encouraged Gough to
'stand like a rock' and boldly advocated the resignations
of other people. But, when he himself wished that he
could find a good reason for resigning, it is permissible
to suspect that the reason would have had to be indeed
compelling before he acted on it. If Gough had not taken
the bull by the horns then, in spite of Wilson, the army in
Ireland would have followed Fergusson's lead.

Carson and Bonar Law were equally certainly mutin-
eers, for they invoked their followers to defy Parliament.
Here again the weight of blame that may fairly be placed
upon them depends on the importance attached to Balfour's
arguments that there are circumstances in which it is
justifiable for a population to resist a Government. But
Asquith's ministry could not be acquitted of responsibility
for this widespread mutiny. It had preferred to con-
centrate on holding together its majority in the House of

o

Commons than to face the fundamental issues of the Anglo-Irish situation.

The Ministers who lost Britain the American colonies asserted, with incontrovertible legality on their side, that those colonies had no right to manufacture so much as a nail for a horseshoe. But the colonies became an independent republic. The Liberals of 1912–14 had all the points of legality on their side, but they never had the slightest chance of forcing Ulster to toe the constitutional line. When, at the eleventh hour, Churchill and Seely sought to do so, their action may be excused on the grounds that it was in response to the most flagrant provocation and that no step they proposed to take was either illegal or one to which loyal subjects of the Crown should object. Nevertheless, it was a rash act. The accusation made against them that they wished to goad the Volunteers into violence so that the Army and Navy might have an excuse for shooting them down and for setting up a military dictatorship was merely symbolic of the hysterical nonsense in · which otherwise sober politicians allowed themselves to indulge.

Their object in setting Paget off along the mazes of his uncertain warpath was, as they repeatedly protested, to save themselves from being made to look fools by the loss of arms and by the taking over of authority in Ulster by the Carsonian private government. They did not issue any specific orders beyond those required to ensure the safety of the depots. But, envisaging as they did, and not without cause, the miscellany of troubles that might have followed had their plan been put into full effect, they inevitably confused and inflamed the emotions of all concerned. They were unlucky in having Paget as their principal agent, but it is the business of statesmen to judge the competence of their agents in advance. Loose talk about the sending of unlimited troops, if the need arose, was dangerous folly, although it had been accompanied by unconvincing assurances that nobody expected need to arise.

Seely and Churchill were treating politics as a game of poker instead of the contract bridge which it more nearly resembles. And they were playing their game, which requires courage in bluffing to be tempered by cool calculations, without regard for the second of these ingredients. Above all, they had failed to consider the consequences of success in their combined naval and military operation. How would it have benefited the Government to hold not only the military bases but the civil buildings in Belfast and all over Ulster? Even if no violence had ensued, which it almost certainly would have done, the will of the Ulstermen to resist would still have had to be taken into account. The old maxim that anything can be done with bayonets except sit on them would have remained true. When they had been ignominiously foiled, the ministers — and now including the Prime Minister — blundered again; their reticence threw a smoke-screen of mystery round the whole affair and laid them open to ugly charges.

One figure emerged unscathed from the closest scrutiny. From beginning to end, the King had shown himself a master of realistic common sense. He intervened up to the limits allowed by the conventions of the day—and never beyond them. Had Victorian convention survived, Asquith would have been saved much humiliation; for the King's grandmother had been allowed — and had wielded without hesitation — far greater influence on her Prime Ministers than was any longer permissible in the new century.

Those hard truths were beginning to come home to the contending parties as they closed their inquest. But how to make a fresh start, how to get out of the impasse by which they were all blocked was another matter. The Irish problem baby still lay squalling on the lap of the mother of Parliaments, and its wails were not to be stilled in the next three months. There were more manœuvrings and more gun-runnings ahead. Hitherto the southern Irish — so regularly in former days the disturbers of the peace of British politics — had been behaving in an unusually exemplary fashion. After an interlude, described in the next chapter, the mutiny was to spread to Dublin.

CHAPTER XV

THE BUCKINGHAM PALACE
CONFERENCE

WITHIN a few days of the great debate the King again showed his hand. On May 1 he told the Speaker that he was prepared to preside at an interparty conference, and the Speaker, Lowther (later Lord Ullswater), expressed his willingness to help. For the next two months the King sought to move Asquith along these lines. He saw the Prime Minister in the middle of May and once more in the middle of June, urging him to take action with the assistance of Lowther. Asquith still did not feel that the time was ripe. He was engaged in yet another series of negotiations behind the scenes. The wooing of Bonar Law and Carson was on again, and it was being conducted in a most amiable fashion. All the leaders were now convinced that, somehow or other, some parts of Ulster must be allowed to contract out. Maps of this and that county began to be exchanged. Asquith, writing to ask Carson to let him have one of these maps which had been prepared in the north, added a postscript to his informal letter. 'I see', he wrote, 'that my late lady friends are transferring their attention to you!' Mrs. Drummond had been making a nuisance of herself on Carson's doorstep.

A few days later, on May 28, Simon, as Attorney-General, invited Carson to his King's birthday dinner. As the bidden guest was still being publicly denounced for the part he had so openly taken in the gun-running, Simon anticipated that there might be some little awkwardness

in accepting the invitation. 'I should be so proud and
pleased if — for old sake's sake — you found it possible
to come. . . . I appreciate you may possibly feel a difficulty (though I trust not) and if you came you would add
greatly to my pleasure. . . . My own feelings of gratitude
and devotion to you for all you did for me never will be
altered, whatever happens.'

But Ulster had tasted blood, and its leaders were no
more optimistic than Redmond had been of getting their
fanatical followers to agree to any concessions. Bonar
Law told Asquith that to try to put through the exclusion
of an area of Ulster was to take a heavy risk. There were
many northerners who felt that the going was so good
that they might still wreck Home Rule as a whole. Asquith
continued to feel his way towards peace ; so unruffled was
he that he tried the patience of the Archbishop of Canterbury. His Grace, coming away from a visit to Downing
Street, told the King's Secretary that he had been annoyed
by the Prime Minister's 'serene optimism and pulseless
attitude'.

Certainly, looking across the water there seemed no
reason for cheerfulness. The Volunteers had carried all
before them and were openly laughing at poor Macready
and his intelligence service. On one occasion when Craig
was telephoning to Richardson, they heard the voice of a
girl at the exchange. 'Quick, Mary, give me the pencil.
Craig and Robertson are going to have a conversation,' she
was saying. 'Wait a bit, Richardson,' said Craig, 'till the
girl has got her pencil from Mary.' Such contemptuous
confidence boded ill for the official appeasers.

They were reinforced by some well-meant unofficial
allies. Lord Murray of Elibank went temporarily into
partnership with Lord Rothermere (the younger brother
of Lord Northcliffe) ; these two saw first the northerners
and then Redmond. They brought to him a scheme for
leaving out an area of Ulster by plebiscite. The counties

and fragments of counties thus excluded were to have been
allowed to stay out without time limit. Bonar Law and
Carson were ready to accept this compromise and, if it
were agreeable to Redmond, to drop their attacks on Home
Rule. Indeed, they promised that they would 'support
and encourage the Irish Parliament in every way'. But
this substantial offer was refused by the Nationalists, who
were still hoping to achieve a united and Home Ruled
Ireland.

Meanwhile some of the academic federalists, headed
by F. S. Oliver, Lionel Curtis and Edward Grigg (later
Lord Altrincham) had seen Bonar Law and the Prime
Minister and put forward the idea of a 'round table'
meeting to work out an Irish national convention to settle
matters on a federal basis. This too came to nothing.
There were forces in London as well as in Belfast prepared
to fight in a die-hard fashion to the last ditch.

Wilson heard from Milner that he was entirely in
favour of the Ulstermen setting up forthwith a provisional
government. 'He is altogether against Ulster waiting any
longer to suit Asquith's convenience and is urgently in
favour of a strong forward policy. He says that of course
the Ulster Government will at first be a "ragged thing"
but there are good men behind it and it will presently get
into working order.' Milner asked Wilson what the army
would do, and was told that 'so much depends on the way
the picture is put to us. I think that if Carson and his
Government were sitting in the City Hall and we were
ordered down to close the Hall, we would not go.' Wilson,
to satisfy himself that this diagnosis of probable army
action was correct, talked it over with Douglas and Sclater,
the successors of French and Ewart. It was a satisfactory
talk. 'I was pleased with the result. They have no
intention at all of moving, except in the ordinary way of
quelling riots.'

Against this background, Parliament was still going

through the motions of bringing the Home Rule Bill nearer to the Statute Book, and, in its now frankly farcical progress, wild words were heard again, in and outside of the Houses.   At the end of May, Carson, speaking to the Covenanters of Wales, jovially taunted the Government for its impotence.   What was happening in Ulster ? — 'Fourteen battleships about Belfast Lough, police drafted in from all parts of Ireland, soldiers confined to their barracks and the Lord Mayor keeping the peace of Belfast, not through the troops but through the Ulster Volunteers.'

At long last Asquith accepted the King's offer and, on July 21, the Conference met at Buckingham Palace. Asquith and Lloyd George attended for the Government, Bonar Law and Lansdowne for the Conservatives, Redmond and Dillon for the Nationalists, and Carson and Craig for the Ulster Unionists.   They met in a large room on the ground floor overlooking the garden, which is easily accessible from the King's private apartments.

The King greeted them with : 'Gentlemen, it is with feelings of satisfaction and happiness that I receive you here today. . . . Any intervention at this moment may be regarded as a new departure. . . . For months we have watched with deep misgivings the course of events in Ireland.   The trend has been surely and steadily towards an appeal to force and today the cry of civil war is on the lips of the most responsible and sober-minded of my people. We have, in the past, endeavoured to act as a civilized example to the world, and to me it is unthinkable, as it must be to you, that we should be brought to the brink of fratricidal strife upon issues apparently so capable of adjustment as these you are now asked to consider, if handled in a spirit of generous compromise.   My apprehension in contemplating such a dire calamity is intensified by my feelings of attachment to Ireland and of sympathy with her people, who have always welcomed me with warmhearted affection.   Gentlemen, you represent in one form or another the vast majority of my subjects at home. You also have a deep interest in my Dominions overseas who are scarcely less concerned in a prompt and friendly settlement of this question. I regard you then in this matter as trustees for the honour and peace of all. Your responsibilities are indeed great. The time is short. . . . I pray that God, in His infinite wisdom, may guide your deliberations.'

Having spoken, the King left, and the Speaker took the chair. They sat for four mornings. It was plain from the start that what the King had said, accurately though it reflected the feelings of a vast majority of the people, would have no practical effect. The differences between the contending parties had now been reduced to the boundaries of the two little counties of Fermanagh and Tyrone. As Churchill reflected later, 'To this pass had the Irish factions in their insensate warfare been able to drive their respective British champions. . . . The north would not agree to this and the south would not agree to that. Both the leaders wished to settle; both had dragged their followers forward to the utmost point they dared. Neither seemed able to give an inch.'

Before this abortive Conference broke up, the King saw each of those who attended it in private audience. At the last the Speaker, who was waiting with Lansdowne and Bonar Law, read in a newspaper the telegram announcing the ultimatum sent by Austria to Serbia. 'I called the attention of my companions to this very serious news which, as our conference had sat early, they had not seen previously and we agreed that it portended some very grave news. How grave we did not then realise.'

There was to be no more 'turning this way and that in search of an exit from the deadlock' (the phrase is Churchill's); the Cabinet was to be spared having any longer to 'toil around the muddy by-ways of Fermanagh and Tyrone'. Churchill must be allowed the last words.

'Since the days of the Blues and the Greens in the Byzantine Empire, partisanship had rarely been carried to more absurd extremes. An all-sufficient shock was, however, at hand.' But before it was delivered and a world war had temporarily banished Ireland back into her mists, another scene was to be played. Before the Germans invaded Belgium, the southern Irish, taking a leaf from the northern book, armed themselves by gun-running.

CHAPTER XVI

THE SOUTH GETS THE GUNS

IT was not to be expected that, with all the marching
and drilling and gun-running going on in the north, the
southern Irish would watch with folded arms. It was
not to be expected, and it did not happen. Redmond had,
throughout the year, been having increasing difficulty in
his patient efforts to keep Irish nationalism on pacific lines.
As the Ulster Volunteers grew, so did the National Volunteers who had had their beginnings in industrial strife and
Larkin's Citizen Army of 1913–14.

So far had Redmond been forced along the unconstitutional path that he sent emissaries to Belgium to
buy rifles. But nothing material might have come of this
had not more daring spirits been moving behind his back.
It is often said that southern Ireland only armed herself in
reply to Larne. This, however, is not borne out by one of
the chief southern gun-runners, a man of letters who had
been caught up into the militant nationalist movement.
Darrell Figgis, in his recollections, which are no less
colourful than those of Crawford, roundly stated that he
and his associates got to work some weeks before the Larne
gun-running and, he went on, 'when the news came from
Larne, we were delighted, and not only because it gave us
an excellent protection from the task at which we were
engaged'.

He and those with him formed a rich contrast of men
and women, some of them Irish and some of them not;
just as northern patriots were joined by English and Scots
sympathizers, so the southerners were reinforced from over

the water. The claim of Ulster citizens to have nothing to do with Home Rule made, as has been seen, a fervent appeal to many of their neighbours in Britain. But others reacted, as British people can always be relied upon to do, in favour of 'a small nation'. Gun-running into Dublin attracted the one type just as similarly lawless adventure had attracted others when the destination was Belfast.

The company of those who joined together to get guns for the south was headed by Roger Casement. He was the Dublin-born son of a captain of Light Dragoons who belonged to an Ulster Protestant family which had come over from the Isle of Man. As events outside the scope of this narrative were soon to prove, he was prepared to go to extreme limits in his zeal for Irish independence and his detestation of British imperialism.

He and others forgathered in the early summer at the house of an elderly lady in the Grosvenor Road. She was Mrs. Green, the Irish-born widow of that highly respectable clergyman and historian, the Rev. J. R. Green. The planners agreed, as had their opposite numbers, that the continental markets must be combed for rifles and bayonets. As the weeks passed, their numbers grew. Two experienced yachtsmen were among them. Robert Erskine Childers, who has already been mentioned as having helped Roberts in putting forward revolutionary views about the use of swords for cavalry in modern warfare, knew as much about the handling of small boats as any man alive. His family connexions were English squires and officers of the Navy and Army, though his mother was Irish. The Erskine Childers who was First Lord of the Admiralty, Secretary for War and Chancellor of the Exchequer in Gladstone's Governments was a first cousin of his father. He had graduated to Irish nationalism from Haileybury, Trinity (Cambridge) and service against the Boers in the South African War.

With him was an old Etonian, Gordon Shephard, who,

for the last few years, had combined the holding of a regular commission in the Royal Fusiliers and in the infant Royal Flying Corps with bold exploring of the strong places round the German coasts. This had involved him in a characteristic interdepartmental squabble between the War Office, the Foreign Office and the Admiralty. He had been arrested by the Germans and released as they could not scrape up enough evidence against him. The Foreign Office had protested to the War Office. Shephard had been rebuked from that quarter and encouraged by the Admiralty to proceed with his seafaring researches while on leave.

The daughter of Lord Monteagle, the Honourable Mary Spring Rice, shipped as a deck hand. Another Spring Rice, Sir Cecil, was at this point of time British Ambassador in Washington. She was not the only lady present, for Mrs. Childers, an American from Boston, also sailed. The head of an ancient clan, the O'Rahilly, came over for the London preparations, reporting that he had been followed by a detective. But, as Figgis recalled, 'London is not Dublin . . . and that night he slept at Hampstead unknown and unguarded'.

If the police were in fact on the trail, they did not seem to have done much about following it up. Figgis and his friends were able to make a tour of the continental black-market centres for arms. Their experiences were remarkably parallel to those of Crawford. They got mixed up with Mexicans and with Jewish dealers. They fell foul of customs men and had to bribe themselves out of trouble by gifts of money and cigars. By the time their plans were maturing, the Larne *coup* had already been brought off and they had some difficulty owing to the mild suspicion that had been aroused in Belgium and Germany. But they got their guns and they wrapped them up in straw. Then, like Crawford before him, Figgis had some anxious moments until his cargo had safely set sail.

There is no record that he took the Almighty into his confidence as Crawford had done, but 'I was able to spend Sunday peacefully in Cologne and hear Beethoven's Mass in D Major in the Cathedral'. Some 1500 Mauser rifles and 49,000 rounds of ammunition were at length shipped from Hamburg. Three yachts were engaged in carrying them to Ireland, the *Asgard* belonging to Erskine Childers, Mr. Conor O'Brien's *Kelpie* and Sir Thomas Myles's *Chotah*. Figgis had never met Conor O'Brien, and so, when the two vessels in which they sailed met in mid-ocean for the transfer of the arms, he was uncertain whether or no he had come up to a stranger. O'Brien put doubts at rest with the hailing shout, 'Is that the boat with the rifles for the Irish Volunteers ?' Figgis was embarrassed, 'calling back in poor Irish asking him to speak in that language, and I was greatly relieved to hear the skipper's low voice asking if this were Mexican'. It is a reasonable supposition that the skipper had had his due share of the cash and the cigars.

Arrangements were made for Childers to land his cargo on the morning of Sunday, July 26, in the little harbour of Howth, which lies a few miles to the north of Dublin. Figgis went ahead so as to be able to go out in a motor-boat and let Childers know that all was plain sailing. If he did not appear, the *Asgard* was to round the coast and enter the mouth of the Shannon. The balance of the cargo was to be taken to St. Tudwal Road off the Welsh coast and there transferred to the *Chotah*. There were hitches, but the main job was done. Figgis had the satisfaction of seeing the yacht, with Mrs. Childers in a red jersey at the helm, coming slowly in. It was broad daylight and there was no attempt at concealment. The Volunteers were there, as they had been in the darkness at Larne.

But there was one official who saw fit to take action against these overt illegal proceedings. He was Mr. David Harrell, the Assistant Commander of Police. 'The White

Yacht, harbinger of Liberty' only seemed to him to be a gun-runner, and he sought to interfere. Figgis told him that to 'march through an Irish city was not illegal, seeing that such a march had been permitted the Sunday before in Belfast City with the Ulster Volunteers'. Figgis, displaying a broad spirit of compromise, agreed that an offence — 'the only offence of the day' — was the illegal landing and 'for that I take entire responsibility'. He offered himself for arrest, stipulating that the arms should be marched off, 'since the right that had been allowed in one Irish city clearly could not, a week later, become an offence in another Irish city'.

This logic did not convince Harrell. He got into touch with Sir James Dougherty, the Under-Secretary in Dublin Castle, but did not tell him that he was calling up the military through General Cuthbert, who commanded an infantry brigade in Dublin. The troops duly appeared on the scene; the arms disappeared, being removed for future use by the Volunteers. But before the troops got back to barracks, blood flowed. A detachment of the King's Own Scottish Borderers, acting in support of the police — a combined operation that had not proved practical in the north — were jeered at and had stones thrown at them by the crowd as they marched through Bachelor's Walk on the quayside of the Liffey. The officer in charge, Major Haigh, changed his rearguard and ordered it to hold the road with fixed bayonets and rifles at the ready. He stated subsequently in evidence that he gave no orders to fire, but firing broke out. Three people were killed and thirty-eight injured.

The consequences of this affair were threefold. First, a scapegoat had to be found, and this proved easy. The zealous Harrell was promptly suspended and a Royal Commission, under Lord Shaw of Dunfermline, appointed to enquire into his behaviour and that of his accomplices. The Commission found that the employment of the police and military was not in accordance with law, and that Harrell was responsible for calling out the military as well as for the orders issued to the police. It acquitted Sir James Dougherty of all blame, but considered that General Cuthbert should have asked himself whether the seizure of arms ‘was invoked by proper authority. ‘Apart from the fundamental illegality as to the seizure of rifles’, the Commissioners reported, ‘they consider that there was no case warranting military intervention. The gathering of the Irish Volunteers and the march through Dublin did not constitute an unlawful assembly requiring dispersal by the military, and their presence or conduct produced no terror to the lieges and it did not endanger life or property or the King’s peace. Between Fairview and Bachelor’s Walk the military were subjected to insult and assaulted with missiles, but in the Commissioners’ opinion, there was no such great and inevitable danger or serious bodily harm as to justify the use of firearms.’ They held it not proved that an actual order to fire was given. The promiscuous firing of rifles by twenty-one soldiers took place without orders, but they thought that the troops were under the impression that the order was given either directly or passed from man to man.

When this remarkable verdict was delivered, it attracted little attention because war had crowded Ireland out of the news. But no sharper reminder could be given of the perils — alike for soldiers and police — of getting mixed up with the maintenance of public order when guns are involved.

Harrell was thus scandalously disposed of, but the consequences of that Sunday’s work were beyond the power of any Royal Commission to control. The south was now armed, even if on a more modest scale than was the north. That was the second consequence. The third was that the cry, ‘Remember Bachelor’s Walk’, was to go echoing through Nationalist Ireland, and to be an effective stimulus to recruiting the Sinn Fein force that was shortly to wrest the leadership from Redmond and his constitutionalist followers. Some of the guns landed at Howth were to be heard during the Easter of 1916 when the seeds of the Irish Republic were germinated in more blood.

But, for the moment, reactions to what had happened at Howth were overshadowed by the outbreak of war. Nothing remained but to ring down the curtain as rapidly as possible on the melodrama of the past two and a half years. There was no longer any question of making another trial of an Amending Bill to make Home Rule acceptable to the Irish as a whole. The main Bill had to be given decent burial, and neither Carson nor Redmond was in any mood to interrupt the ceremony. Carson put his Volunteers and their weapons (including the early dummy ones which came in useful for training Kitchener's army) at the disposal of the Government. Redmond, for his part, gave an assurance (which he was, by this time, in no position to implement) that troops might be withdrawn from Ireland, the coasts of which would be 'defended from foreign invasion by her armed sons'.

The funeral of the Third Home Rule Bill was arranged to take place in two parts. The battle-scarred original was to go on to the Statute Book and, with it, a Suspensory Bill, postponing the operation of Home Rule until the war had ended. Redmond loyally accepted this postponement and did his best to persuade a suspicious War Minister in the person of Kitchener, and a no less suspicious War Office, that the young men of the south should be encouraged to join up and be allowed to see active service together as a division. On September 18 Parliament was prorogued, and on that day the Royal Assent was signified to the Home Rule and the Welsh Church Bills. There was one principal absentee in an otherwise full House. Carson was not in his place; on the day before he had been married

P

for the second time. The wedding had been held quietly
in the parish church of Charlton Musgrove in Somerset.

'The Government of Ireland Act', said the Clerk on the
Opposition side of the table. 'Le Roi le veult', said the
Clerk on the Ministerial side, bowing to the Lord Chancellor; the time-honoured phrase has seldom sounded
with more ironic overtones. A long roll of cheering was
heard from the Commons at the Bar, and in the side
galleries. In the Lower House, when the Deputy-Speaker
was leaving the chair, Will Crooks asked him if it would be
in order for the House to sing 'God Save the King'.
Crooks did not wait for a reply, and the National Anthem
was sung. Crooks then called for three cheers and, as they
died away, he called out 'God Save Ireland'. Redmond,
in response, cried 'God Save England'.

So the curtain fell on Home Rule. It was never to rise
again. The pantomime battle had ended. Redmond's
'God Save England' were the last words of the Nationalist
Party. For more than a century Irish members had added
to the confusion and to the gaiety of successive parliaments.
When next a new parliament assembled to face the hazards
of peace, southern Ireland had turned her back on Westminster. Those who held power in the south preferred to
appeal to the gun and to laugh at the British ballot-box.
They owed much to the militant example of Ulster. The
Sinn Fein dream of a Republic might never have come true
had matters been ordered differently in Britain and Ireland
between 1912 and 1914.

CHAPTER XVII

HOW THEY LIVED THEREAFTER

THE writers of old melodramatic novels observed the satisfying custom of rounding off their three-deckers with a brief account of what happened to the characters, especially the minor ones, after the story ended. Such a postscript seems appropriate to this political melodrama played at Westminster, Belfast and the Curragh.

Seely was given a staff appointment by French, who, restored to favour when the First World War broke out, commanded the Expeditionary Force. But the staff was too tame for him and he was soon at the head of a Canadian cavalry brigade. The appointment brought him under Gough and they became great friends. Surviving the war, he became Under-Secretary of State for Air and once flew to the House of Commons by seaplane. He lived to a ripe old age, surviving, happy and busy, until 1947.

Gough, after proving himself as a fighting general and commanding the 5th Army, fell victim to the politicians who had failed to unseat him at the Curragh. But, undaunted, he has enjoyed a varied career in business, and lived to command the Home Guard in Chelsea and to look back with relish on all the episodes of his past.

Fergusson, having served with distinction as a corps commander until the end of the war, unsuccessfully contested a Scottish seat as a Conservative and then, in 1924, went out to New Zealand as Governor-General and Commander-in-Chief. There he was happy, popular and successful; he died in 1951.

Paget, having fallen foul of French, did not get the command of the army corps which he had expected. But he was able to get a brother guardsman appointed in his place. Then he was chosen as British representative at headquarters; French again stood in his path. He never got an overseas command. On retirement he devoted himself to gardening, golf and other hobbies.

Wilson was appointed Chief Liaison Officer at the headquarters of his old allies, the French. Later, he commanded an army corps, and then, having won the favour of Lloyd George, who appreciated his pliant fluency, he was made Chief of the Imperial General Staff to supersede the blunt, outspoken Robertson. He opposed British participation in the League of Nations; he was promoted Field-Marshal; he was created a baronet; he received the thanks of Parliament and a grant of £10,000; he was elected Conservative member of Parliament for a northern Irish constituency. On June 22, 1922, he unveiled the war memorial of the Great Eastern Railway Company at the entrance to Liverpool Street Station. Returning in a taxi from this ceremony to his house in Eaton Place, he found himself, on getting out, attacked by two young men with revolvers. He was in uniform; he turned and drew his sword. Two bullets entered his chest, and when Lady Wilson, who had heard the noise and the hall door being thrown open by a servant, came out, he was dying. His assassins, both Irishmen and one a cripple with a wooden leg, were armed with service revolvers and service ammunition. They were hanged.

The gun-runners were treated diversely by fate. Crawford refused £1000 which his grateful countrymen offered him for his gun-running. When the King and Queen visited Belfast in 1921, he was included in the Royal Honours List and decorated with the C.B.E. He lived until 1952, facing with serenity the blindness that afflicted him in later years. His daughter, Bethia, whose name the *Fanny* had temporarily borne, married a Commander in the Royal Navy, and his other daughter, Doreen, whose name had similarly been borrowed, married a diplomatist in the British Service.

Casement, in November 1914, got into Germany (from America), where he tried to seduce British prisoners of war of Irish descent to join an Irish Brigade and to fight against Britain. He was unsuccessful. Then in the spring of 1916 he persuaded the Germans to send him to Ireland in a submarine to organize rebellion. He was captured, tried for high treason and hanged at Pentonville Prison, where his body lies in spite of periodic efforts on the part of the Irish Government to have it exhumed and buried in Ireland.

Childers served with the Royal Naval Air Service and won the D.S.C. He then threw himself into the thick of the Irish troubles as an uncompromising Sinn Feiner. He refused to accept the first settlement with the British and joined de Valera's Republicans against the newly formed Free State Government. He was ambushed by Free State soldiers and, although he was armed, he did not fire because a woman threw herself between him and his opponents. He was court-martialled and shot at Beggar's Bush barracks in 1922 (four months after Wilson's murder) by a firing party of his adopted countrymen; he shook hands with each member of it. His son has held office as the only Protestant Cabinet minister in de Valera's Government.

Darrell Figgis, who took part in the Irish 'Troubles', was elected a member of the Dail. Borne down by private troubles, he committed suicide in a gas-filled room in Bloomsbury in 1925.

Shephard was killed in the crash of an aeroplane he was piloting at the beginning of 1918; by then he had risen to the rank of Brigadier-General.

Redmond died suddenly, a few months before the end

of the war; he had lived to know that the Easter Rebellion had shattered his hopes of a peaceful settlement of the Irish question.

F. E. Smith — Galloper Smith, who had ridden with Carson — wrote a friendly and amusing preface to Seely's autobiography. His galloping against the Constitution forgotten, he lived to enjoy the most glittering of legal prizes, the Lord Chancellorship.

Carson joined Asquith's coalition in May 1915 as a law officer, being appointed Attorney-General. He resigned in October 1916 and took an active part in the manœuvres that led to the fall of Asquith and to the formation of the Lloyd George ministry. He joined it in Churchill's old office — as First Lord of the Admiralty. His Volunteers went to France as the Ulster Division and, at Thiepval and in other famous actions, covered themselves with glory.

And Churchill — so far as it is given to mortal man to do so — lived happily ever after.

BIBLIOGRAPHY OF PUBLISHED SOURCES

ACKNOWLEDGMENT to those to whom I am indebted for verbal recollections and for access to unpublished materials is made in the Preface.

Use has been made of *The Dictionary of National Biography*, the *Annual Register* and of the files of *The Times*, *Morning Post*, *Daily Telegraph*, *Westminster Gazette*, *Round Table*, *Contemporary Review*, *Illustrated London News*.

Amery, L. S. *My Political Life*. Vol. I : *England Before the Storm, 1896–1914*. London. Hutchinson. 1953.

Asquith, H. H. (the Earl of Oxford and Asquith). *Fifty Years of Parliament*. Vol. II. London. Cassell. 1926.

— *Memories and Reflections*. Vols. I and II. London. Cassell. 1928.

Beaverbrook, Lord. *Politicians and the War, 1914–16*. London. Thornton Butterworth. 1928.

Birkenhead, The Earl of. *Frederick Edwin, Earl of Birkenhead. The First Phase*. London. Thornton Butterworth. 1933.

Butler, Sir William. *An Autobiography*. London. Constable. 1911.

Callwell, Major-General Sir C. E. *Field-Marshal Sir Henry Wilson. His Life and Diaries*. Vol. I. London. Cassell. 1927.

Carty, James. *Ireland from the Great Famine to the Treaty (1851–1921. A Documentary Record*. Dublin. Fallon. 1951.

— *Bibliography of Irish History, 1912–21*. Dublin. Stationery Office. 1936.

Childs, Major-General Sir Wyndham. *Episodes and Reflections*. London. Cassell. 1930.

Churchill, Winston S. *The World Crisis, 1911–14*. London. Thornton Butterworth. 1923.

Colvin, Ian. *The Life of Lord Carson*. (3 volumes. Vol. I, by Edward Marjoribanks). London. Gollancz. 1932, 1934, 1936.

Cooper, Duff. *Haig*. Vol. I. London. Faber & Faber. 1935.

Crawford, Fred. H. (Lieut.-Colonel). *Guns For Ulster*. Belfast. Printed by Graham & Heslip. 1947.

Dugdale, Blanche E. C. *Arthur James Balfour*. Vols. I and II. London. Hutchinson. 1936 and 1936.

Dunlop, Colonel John K. *The Development of the British Army, 1899–1914.* London. Methuen. 1938.

Ensor, R. C. K. *England, 1870–1914.* Oxford, at the Clarendon Press. 1936.

Figgis, Darrell. *Recollections of the Irish War.* London. Benn. 1927.

French, Major the Hon. Gerald. *The Life of Field-Marshal Sir John French.* London. Cassell. 1931.

Gleichen, Major-General Lord Edward. *A Guardsman's Memories.* Edinburgh and London. Blackwell. 1932.

Gough, General Sir Hubert. *Soldiering On.* London. Arthur Barker. 1954.

Graham, Colonel Henry. *History of the Sixteenth, the Queen's, Light Dragoons (Lancers) 1912–25.* Devizes. Privately printed by George Simpson. 1936.

Gwynn, Denis. *The Life of John Redmond.* London. Harrap. 1932.

Gwynn, Stephen. *The History of Ireland.* London and Dublin. Macmillan. 1932.

Hammond, J. L. *Gladstone and the Irish Nation.* London. Longmans, Green. 1938.

—— *C. P. Scott of the Manchester Guardian.* London. Bell. 1934.

Harvey, Colonel J. R. *The History of the 5th (Royal Irish) Regiment of Dragoons from 1689 to 1799, afterwards the 5th Royal Irish Lancers from 1858 to 1921.* For private circulation only. Aldershot. Printed by Gale & Polden. 1923.

Healy, T. M. *Letters and Leaders of My Day.* Vol. II. London. Thornton Butterworth. 1928.

Horgan, J. J. *Parnell to Pearse.* Dublin. Browne & Nolan. 1948.

Howell, Mrs. *Philip Howell.* London. Allen & Unwin. 1942.

Hyde, H. Montgomery. *Carson.* London. Heinemann. 1953.

James, David. *Lord Roberts.* London. Hollis & Carter. 1954.

Lochliamm, Colm O. *Irish Street Ballads.* Dublin. At the Sign of the Three Candles in Fleet Street. 1952.

Lyons, F. S. L. *The Irish Parliamentary Party, 1890–1910.* London. Faber & Faber. 1951.

Macardle, Dorothy. *The Irish Republic. A Documented Chronicle of the Anglo-Irish Conflict.* 4th Edition. Dublin. Irish Press Ltd. 1951.

Macdonagh, Michael. *The Life of William O'Brien.* London. Benn. 1928.

McNeill, Ronald. *Ulster's Stand For Union.* London. Murray. 1922.

Macready, General the Rt. Hon. Sir Nevil. *Annals of an Active Life*. Vols. I and II. London. Hutchinson. 1924.

Maurice, Major-General Sir Frederick. *Haldane, 1856–1915*. London. Faber & Faber. 1937.

Midleton, The Earl of. *Ireland — Dupe or Heroine*. London. Heinemann. 1932.

Newton, Lord. *Lord Lansdowne*. London. Macmillan. 1929.

Nicolson, Harold. *King George V*. London. Constable. 1952.

O'Brien, William. *Evening Memories*. Dublin. Maunsel. 1920.

O'Flaherty, Liam. *The Life of Tim Healy*. London. Cape. 1927.

O'Hegarty, P. S. *A History of Ireland Under the Union, 1801–1922*. London. Methuen. 1952.

Petrie, Sir Charles. *Life and Letters of the Rt. Hon. Sir Austen Chamberlain*. Vol. I. London. Cassell. 1939.

Riddell, Lord. *More Pages From My Diary, 1908–1914*. London. Country Life Ltd. 1934.

Robertson, Field-Marshal Sir William. *From Private to Field-Marshal*. London. Constable. 1921.

Seely, Major-General the Rt. Hon. J. E. B. *Adventure*. London. Heinemann. 1930.

Shephard, Brigadier-General Gordon. *Memoirs*. London. Privately Printed. 1924.

Spender, J. A., and Asquith, Cyril. *Life of Herbert Henry Asquith, Lord Oxford and Asquith*. Vols. I and II. London. Hutchinson. 1932.

Ullswater, The Rt. Hon. James William Lowther, Viscount. *A Speaker's Commentaries*. Vols. I and II. London. Arnold. 1925.

Winterton, Earl. *Orders of the Day*. London. Cassell. 1953.

— *Pre-War*. London. Macmillan. 1932.

INDEX

Agar-Robartes, T. C., 46
Agnew, Andy, 173, 175, 176, 177, 178, 181
Aitken, Max (later Lord Beaverbrook), 75, 86-7
'All for Ireland' league, 19
Allenby, Major-General Edmund (later Lord), 128
American Irish, 4, 26
Amery, L. S., 23, 122
Ancient Order of Hibernians, 42, 46, 73, 112
Anglesey, Marquis of (as Earl of Uxbridge), 105
Ardagh, Sir John, 101
Armagh, Archbishop of, 69
Arms : seizures, 70 ; royal proclamation prohibiting import and coastwise carriage, 92-3 ; reported plots to raid stores, 117 ; Cabinet committee, 117-18 ; Army Council commands for precautions, 118 ; gun-running, 169, 170-82, 188, 201, 202, 203-7
Asgard, gun-running by, 204
Asquith, H. H. (later Earl of Oxford and Asquith), xiii, xv, xvi, xvii, 1, 3, 5-6, 8, 11-12, 15, 20, 29, 43-5, 51, 64-5, 76, 79, 82, 84, 85-6, 88, 89, 90, 103, 115-16, 120, 122, 138, 147, 148, 156, 159-60, 164, 165, 167, 169, 190, 193, 196, 197, 198, 212 ; letter from King, 35-6 ; visit to Ireland, 47-9 ; decision against putting criminal law in motion against Carson, 74 ; interview and exchange of letters with King, 78-9, 80 ; interview with King and meetings with Bonar Law, 86-7 ; talks with Carson, 89 ; talks with Bonar Law and Carson, 91, 93-4 ; interview with King, 110 ; approach to Carson, 113 ; interview with Redmond, 113-14 ; further approach to Carson, 114 ;

letter of complaint from King, 148 ; statement to *The Times*, 151, 169 ; becomes War Minister, 159 ; interviews with King, 195 ; negotiations with Bonar Law and Carson, 195, 196 ; Buckingham Palace Conference, 198-9
Asquith, Margot, xiii, 160-1

Balfour, A. J. (later Earl of Balfour), 31, 49, 67, 68-9, 72, 77, 79, 96, 156, 163-4, 165, 188
Balmarino, 178, 179
Banbury, Sir Frederick, 65
Beaverbrook, Lord (as Max Aitken). *See* Aitken, Max
Belfast, Dean of (later Bishop of Down), 62
Belfast : McCann case, 7-8 ; application for leave to drill Orange Lodges, 30-1 ; Churchill's intention to speak at Ulster Hall denounced, 32-3 ; Celtic Park football ground chosen for speech, 33-35 ; demonstration attended by Bonar Law and some seventy M.P.s, 40-2, 44-5 ; reprisals against Castledawson procession affair, 47 ; Celtic Park riot, 56 ; Ulster Hall meeting on Covenant, 61 ; arms seizure, 70 ; insurance coverage, 71 ; July 12 procession, 73 ; proposed occupation of Government Buildings, 136-7 ; Ulster Unionist Council document on plans for police possession of Old Town Hall, 167
Belfast confetti, 47
Beresford, Lord Charles, 164, 188, 190
Bethia. See Fanny
Birrell, Augustine, 8, 15, 46-7, 76-7, 90, 110, 114, 115, 117, 118, 164
Blenheim, demonstrators invited to, 49-52

THE END

PRINTED BY R. & R. CLARK, LTD., EDINBURGH